The
Garden
Buildings
Manual

Published in September 2007

British Library Cataloguing in Publication Data:
A catalogue record for this book is available from the British Library

ISBN 1 84425 352 4

Published by Haynes Publishing, Sparkford, Yeovil,
Somerset BA22 7JJ, UK
Tel: 01963 442030 Fax: 01963 440001
Int. tel: +44 1963 442030 Int. fax: +44 1963 440001
E-mail: sales@haynes.co.uk
Website: www.haynes.co.uk

Haynes North America Inc.
861 Lawrence Drive, Newbury Park,
California 91320, USA

Printed and bound in Great Britain by J. H. Haynes & Co. Ltd, Sparkford

While every effort is taken to ensure the accuracy of the information given in this book, no liability can be accepted by the author or publishers for any loss, damage or injury caused by errors in, or omissions from, the information given.

Acknowledgements

Thanks to Carol, for her assistance and patience whilst I was writing this book; Dave, for his ever-present support and advice; Louise McIntyre and Ian Heath at Haynes for their patience; Jon Web of Natural England for his advice on insect hibernation; the RSPB for the basic nesting box designs, and for vetting the boxes; Brian and friends for the use of their gardens; Cadbury the dog and Midge and Smokey the rabbits for their services as models; and the many suppliers who provided guidance, advice and materials, especially Abru, Bahco, Black & Decker, Cuprinol, Evode, Finnforest, Hales & Co (Drybrook), Henkel, Masterplug, Metpost, OSC Olympic, Sadolin and Stanley Tools.

Tony Lush
February 2007

The Garden Buildings Manual

Tony Lush BA MSc

CONTENTS

GETTING STARTED

This chapter provides the essential background information you'll need for the tasks set out in the rest of the book. Please don't skip the section on safety: it may seem a boring subject, but it's essential that you work safely. Some of the project descriptions suggest additional recommended precautions where they either differ from the considerations set out below or need to be emphasised. However, safety is a little like personal hygiene: it's up to you!

Each of the five project chapters follows a similar format. Though the suggestions regarding material requirements are as accurate as possible, you're strongly recommended not to follow these to the letter. It's far better if you measure up for yourself and work out what you need. The timber used will vary in size and this will effect the overall dimensions.

The tool list covers all the tools that I used during construction.

The procedure for each job is divided into steps which, in most cases, are set out in chronological order. However, you may prefer to follow a different sequence. Take the time to read the instructions for each step before doing the job, since they contain tips and other advice. It's especially important to check for accuracy constantly as you proceed – remember the old adage 'measure twice and cut once'!

Safety

Working safely should be a habit, not an afterthought. Consider the job you're about to do, try to foresee any hazards and make plans to avoid them.

Electrical safety
Make sure all electrical equipment is in good order, especially extension leads and mains leads on power tools.

■ Before using an extension lead, check that the sheathing isn't damaged. If it is, throw the lead away and buy a new one.

■ The plug or socket must be undamaged and must be properly connected with the lead sheath clamped under the cord grip in the plug.
■ Extension leads are for temporary use only. When used the lead must be run in such a way that it cannot get damaged.
■ Ensure the lead is fully unwound from the reel.
■ Plug the lead into an RCD (trip) just in case.

Tool safety
All tools must be in good repair, used as they're intended to be used, and in a fit condition – that is, not blunt or damaged.

■ Read and understand the safety instructions for any tools and materials used. These will inform you of the appropriate personal protective equipment (PPE) that should be used.
■ Keep the work area tidy – try not to have tools and offcuts of timber all over the floor.
■ Remove nails or screws from used timber.
■ Wear suitable clothing, nothing too loose – beware especially of baggy sleeves. Tie back long hair, and wear stout shoes, not sandals.
■ Keep children and pets away from the work area.
■ Lift heavy items with care and with the help of as many people as needed.
■ Clamp the piece you're working on either to the bench or to a firm base.
■ Use ladders safely and properly. When you buy a ladder there'll be instructions on it – follow them. If in doubt try my website.

Personal protective equipment (PPE)
■ Wear gloves when working with treated timber.
■ Wear safety glasses when sawing, drilling, screwing, or applying timber treatment.
■ Follow manufacturers' safety recommendations for all materials and tools.
■ Wear a dust mask when sanding or sawing or when working in a dusty environment.
■ Wear ear defenders when working with noisy equipment.

First Aid kit

Always have a well-stocked First Aid kit handy and ensure people know where it is. The list below is not exhaustive, but it's a good start. But remember: the best First Aid precaution is to work safely.

A First Aid kit should not contain medication or tablets but should include a pencil and paper and the local surgery and pharmacy phone numbers. In addition there should be:

- 20 assorted plasters
- 5 antiseptic wipes (alcohol free)
- 1 eyewash solution (20ml)
- 2 sterile eye pads
- 2 large sterile dressing pads (18 x 18cm)
- 6 safety pins
- 2 triangular bandages (calico)
- 2 medium sterile dressing pads (12 x 12cm)
- 2 crepe roller bandages (7.5cm x 4.5m)
- Hypoallergenic tape (1.25cm x 9.2m)
- 4 pairs vinyl gloves (medium)
- Plastic tweezers
- 1 pair of scissors
- 1 forehead strip thermometer
- 1 disposable face shield
- 1 emergency foil blanket

(For the British Red Cross's recommended domestic First Aid kit see **www.redcross.org.uk**)

In addition to this kit, ensure that you have personal protective equipment that's easy to find and in good working order. The minimum requirements are safety glasses, dust mask, ear defenders, and gloves.

Regulations

The following section is a brief overview of the regulations and requirements that apply to the constructions covered in this book. It is *not* a definitive list – if you have any doubts at all contact the appropriate authority before you start work.

Planning permission

The only constructions in this book that may require planning permission are the shed, the decking, and the greenhouse. If you're in any doubt about whether or not you need permission, contact your Local Authority planning department. If you live in a listed building or in a conservation area then it's especially wise to check what you can and cannot build. Try visiting the Government website at **www.communities.gov.uk**.

Planning permission will *probably* not be required for the shed or greenhouse constructed in chapters 5 and 6. This is because sheds are usually included in the 'permitted development' category. However, there are a few regulations of which you need to be aware. You *will* need planning permission if:

- The shed will cover more than half the land around the house.
- The shed will be used for business purposes.
- The shed is more than 3m high (or 4m if it has a ridge roof).
- The house/garden is a listed building.
- The shed is in a conservation area and more than 10m³ in volume (if the shed is 2m wide and 2m high, it needs to be more than 2.5m long before it falls within this size range).
- There are any restrictions in the planning permission for the property.
- The shed/greenhouse is closer to any highway than the nearest part of the original house, unless this distance is more than 20m.

If there is any doubt about whether or not planning permission is needed, consult your local planning office.

Planning permission requirements for decking

The Timber Decking Association (TDA) at **www.tda.co.uk** publishes a free leaflet (Ref TB 02) outlining the Planning and Building Regulations that apply to decks. Most – but not all – decking structures are exempt from planning regulations, but permission may be required in some cases. These include:

- Where the deck is situated within 20m of a highway.
- Where the deck is at first floor level or above.
- If any part of the deck construction exceeds 3m in height.
- If the structure would adversely affect the value or privacy of neighbouring properties.
- If the deck is attached to a listed building or situated in a conservation area or a national park.

With the exception of ground level decks, property owners should always check that planning regulations do not apply to their proposed structure.

Building Regulations

The only item in this book that that may be subject to Building Regulations could be the decking, and then only if it's high up.

Building Regulations control most aspects of construction, including electricity and drainage. Sheds and greenhouses are exempt from the structural requirements of the Building Regulations, but are not free from the electrical wiring aspect (Part P) nor drainage considerations if drainage is required.

Step and stair construction could require Building Regulations approval if the deck is high. These state that the steps should be at least 910mm (36in) wide. The rise (vertical distance between steps) should be no more than 190mm (7½in), and the depth of a tread (going) at least 254mm (10in). Building codes will also govern how the stair is supported and attached, and whether or not you need a railing.

Part K of the regulations stipulates the design of balustrades for stairs and elevated structures.

Electricity

All electrical work must comply with Part P of the Building Regulations, which states that electrical installations require a test certificate completed by a suitably qualified person – a member of NAPIT (**www.napit.org.uk**), for example. See **www.communities.gov.uk** for additional details.

The regulations for electrical wiring in garden sheds, and greenhouses is particularly strict. 'IP' ratings indicate how resistant to weather a fitting is: the higher the number, the more resistant the fitting. Fittings with a rating lower than IP56 should not be used outside unless this is recommended by the manufacturer.

Glass

There are very strict regulations about the use of glass in habitable buildings but none that I can find regarding the glass used in greenhouses. Horticultural glass is usually 3mm thick and comes in various sizes. The greenhouse described in Chapter 6 will use panes measuring 610 x 610mm and 1422 x 730mm.

For more details visit **www.double-glazing-uk.co.uk**.

You may feel that it's a wise precaution to fit safety glass in the door and in areas close to the door.

Water

All plumbing must comply with the Water Supply (water fittings) Regulations and Byelaws 2000 (see **http://www.southernwater.co.uk**, **www.wras.co.uk**, and **www.defra.gov.uk**.

There are strict requirements for the installation of an outside tap. In brief, the tap must be insulated against freezing, must be able to be isolated in the house, must have a double-check valve in the pipework somewhere, and should be able to be drained to empty the pipework.

Design considerations

This section covers the very basic considerations of design – it is not a diatribe on aesthetics.

Roofs

If you're building a shed or a greenhouse consider the angle of the roof. This is usually the angle at the bottom of the rafters, but it could be taken at the apex. Ideally, it should match the roof angle of the other buildings in the area. However, this isn't always feasible. To get an idea if the angle looks right, lay pieces of timber out on the ground or fix them to a wall and adjust the angle until you find the one that looks best to you.

To measure the angle of the roof, hold a long spirit level horizontal at the base of the roof and set a sliding bevel to the angle of the roof or bargeboard. The angle can then be established using a protractor or by cutting the angle on a chop saw.

The roof angle could be measured at the apex. This is the way the angle of the greenhouse roof was established. The angle at the apex, between the two rafters, was set on a sliding bevel. This was then marked onto a piece of thin card and cut out.

The card was then folded in half. The resulting angle is the angle at the top of the rafters.

Gutters and rainwater butts

Guttering is an important feature of some buildings, partly because it protects the walls from water running off the roof and partly because it changes the look of a building. So take care you select appropriate guttering.

Before applying the guttering, plan where the outfall water will be directed. It needs to be directed into existing gullies, into a soakaway dug for the purpose, or to an area that can cope with large quantities of water.

In addition there's the environmental aspect of collecting rainwater in a butt for use on the garden. Even if a butt is fitted, it's still necessary to plan where the excess water will go.

Door sizes

One consideration when designing the greenhouse and the shed was the width and height of the door – it's so important to be able to get in and out easily and to be able to move the lawnmower, bicycle, wheelbarrow, or whatever without having to become a contortionist! One specific requirement for the greenhouse was that there should be no step-over sill in the doorway, as there had been in the old aluminium greenhouse it replaced.

It may be that the doorway can be constructed so that it'll accept an 'off-the-peg' door – this will save a lot of work building a one-off door to fit.

Consider which way the door is to open. Convention has it that it should open outwards, but convention is there to be reinterpreted.

Window sizes

Windows in a garden building are often there just to let in a little light. However, if your building has a particular purpose the windows may need to be a design factor. One aspect to consider is that the windows don't interfere with the way the shed is used. For instance, there's no point fitting a large window if the shed is intended for storage.

Animals' requirements

Any habitat built for an animal must satisfy that animal's needs, especially if it is captive. Birds won't nest in a box that's not right for them, hedgehogs won't enter a habitat that they dislike, and bats will certainly shun unsuitable boxes. In addition, the choice of timber preservative – if any – is also crucial to the wellbeing of the inhabitant.

When it comes to designing habitats for domestic animals, such as rabbits or dogs, more care needs to be taken. Ask advice about design requirements and don't ignore the advice given. Both the rabbit hutch and the kennel have been constructed to the recommended sizes and styles. Having said that, there's no need to ignore additional design possibilities – it's great to allow your imagination free rein as long as the basics have been considered.

Steps

Steps need to be comfortable and safe. In some cases, such as for steps up to a high deck, Building Regulations will have an input regarding their design, but in other cases it's a matter of choice. If you can, try a set of steps that has already been built. If they're comfortable to use, measure the height of the step (riser) and the depth of the step tread (going), since it's these that make the step comfortable or otherwise.

Try to get all the risers the same height. It's surprising how off-putting it is to have even a small 15mm change in riser height in a flight of steps.

Timber treatments

Safety

Timber treatment materials are being increasingly well regulated. Regardless of that, they still need to be used safely and carefully.

Gloves are recommended when working with treated timber, as much to prevent splinters as to protect your hands against the chemicals used. However, you should *always* wash your hands after handling treated timber.

Don't leave containers of timber treatment where it can be reached by children or animals.

Follow the manufacturers' instructions carefully and be certain to use the correct product for the job in hand.

Creosote and other coal tar products were banned for use by the public in June 2003. If you still have any, don't use it: ask you Local Authority how to dispose of it.

CCA (chromated copper arsenate) based preservatives were banned for general use by an EU directive in June 2004. One of the replacements for CCAs is Tanalith E. All the replacements have fewer harmful chemicals and certainly no arsenic. Contact Arch Timber Protection (01977 714000) for more details.

It's also recommended that treated timber is not burned in the home or on a bonfire. Take it to your local recycling facility to get rid of it.

Environmental considerations

According to Arch Timber Protection, Tanalith E is safe to use on nesting boxes, bat boxes, and plant edging. The chemicals do tend to leach out from the timber a little, but at least it's not leaching out arsenic.

Finnforest supply a timber called Thermowood which needs no preservative – it is heat-treated in a kiln and as a result is resistant to decay. This sounds ideal for use in decking as well as animal habitats, especially for animals that are susceptible to preservatives.

Application – spray, brush, soak, pressure

Follow the manufacturers' instructions carefully. If possible stand the cut end of a length of timber in a container of the treatment and allow it to soak up for the recommended time. Failing that, apply a liberal coat of preservative to the cut timber with a brush. Spraying does work but needs to be done with great care and adherence to the manufacturer's instructions. Application with a brush or roller is satisfactory.

Always apply timber treatment to any cut in treated timber, including any holes drilled into it – in fact, treat any timber that has been worked.

Most pre-treated timber has been processed in a pressurised tank of preservative so that the treatment is forced into the fibres of the wood. This is a far more effective method than can be achieved at home.

Timber treatments used in this book

Cuprinol – Shed and Fence Preserver; Garden Wood Preserver. Cuprinol 5 Star (which has been reformulated recently) was used as a clear treatment when the timber was left in its original state and not coloured strongly. Sadolin – Classic Light Oak; Extra Durable Clear Coat; Opaque Wood Protection, Jungle Green.

Fixings

All fixings used for construction in the garden must be rust resistant. There are various ways of achieving this: one is to use a material that doesn't rust, such as stainless steel, brass, aluminium, or copper; another, and the more usual way, is to use a fixing that's been plated by means of galvanising, 'bright zinc plating' (BZP), or anodising (black japanning is not suitable). Though I'm informed that BZP screws are rust resistant, in my experience they're not.

Since the plating on fixings used in treated timber can be corroded by the preservative it's important to use fixings that have been plated suitably.

Screws

We still size screws largely using imperial measurements, *ie* by inches and gauge (g). A screw that's 2in long and has a gauge of 10 is referred to as a 2in x 10g. The way the gauge is achieved is immaterial to this book: it's sufficient to know that the larger the gauge, the bigger the diameter of the screw. Metric screws, however, are becoming more widely available.

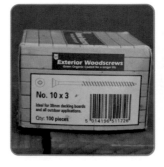

Imperial to metric conversion table

Imperial gauge	Metric gauge
4	3.0
6	3.5
8	4.0
10	5.0
12	5.5
14	6.0

It's good practice to drill clearance holes for screws so that they go into the timber easily, and a pilot hole to encourage the screw to go into the wood and help stop the wood splitting. Sometimes a counterbore is useful so that the head of the screw can rest below the surface.

Recommended drill sizes

Screw gauge	Clearance hole size (mm)	Pilot hole size (mm)	Counterbore size (mm)
4g	3.5	2	6
6g	4	2	7
8g	5	2.5	9
10g	6	3	10
12g	6.5	3	11

Screw head recesses

The type of screwdriver bit required is dependent on the type of recess in the screw head. There is a wide and confusing variety of these, but the three encountered most often are slot head (becoming hard to buy, possibly due to the influx of power-screwdrivers), which require an ordinary slot screwdriver; and two distinct types of cross-head: Posidriv screws, which need a Posidriv screwdriver bit or an RCH (recessed cross head) bit, *not* a Phillips bit; and Phillips screws, which need a Phillips screwdriver bit, *not* a Posidriv one. About the only screws that have a Phillips recess are drywall screws. Posidriv and Phillips screwdrivers each have three commonly used bit sizes – 1, 2 and 3.

Posidriv screwdriver bit size table

Imperial screw gauge	Metric screw gauge	Posidriv bit size
4	3.0	1
6	3.5	2
8	4.0	2
10	5.0	2
12	5.5	3
14	6.0	4

There is one other recess type mentioned in this book: the FastenMaster deck screws mentioned in Chapter 3 need a No 2 square screwdriver bit. These can be bought from Trend.

Screw head shapes

In addition to different recesses there are different shapes of screw head. You will find three different shapes used in this book: countersunk, hexagonal, and pan.

Countersunk screws are the most common wood screws, and as their name suggests they're intended to be countersunk below the surface. This can, and should, be done using a countersink bit to open out the top of the drill hole. However, cordless screwdrivers are so powerful they drive the screw below the surface easily. This presents the problem of getting the screws out, because when they're driven in the wood covers the head of the screw, but when they're removed this wood is forced out in splinters.

Pan-head screws are usually self-tapping – more on these later.

Hexagonal-headed screws are usually coach screws (see below). These can be driven in using a hand-operated spanner or a hexagonal bit fitted into a powered screwdriver.

Materials for screws

Most screws are made from steel of some type. Stainless steel screws are available but are expensive. They're ideal when the screw needs to be very rust resistant and tough.

Brass screws snap rather easily, especially if you're using a power-screwdriver. To avoid some of the problems, drive a steel screw of the same size into the hole first, then remove the screw and drive in the brass one either by hand or with the torque setting on the drill/driver set quite low.

Types of screw

Coach screws have a hexagonal head and can be driven in using a spanner. However, there's now a separate variety available that is not, strictly speaking, a coach screw. These tend to be called by a

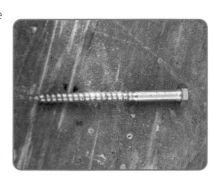

manufacturer's name rather than a generic term. One type used in this book are called DeckBolts, which can have a variety of heads and tend to be a lot smaller in diameter than coach screws.

Self-tapping screws are ideal for screwing into sheet metal. A pilot hole of the correct size is first drilled, and as the screw is driven into the hole it cuts a thread that grips in the metal.

Nails

Rust-resistant nails are usually galvanised. The principal varieties of nail are: round wire nails, which have a round shank and a pronounced head; oval nails, which have an oval shank and a head that's small enough to drive below the surface of timber; and clout nails, which have a large head and are ideal for fixing felt (the short ones are often referred to as felt nails), and, sometimes, feather-edge timber if the head isn't showing.

What size nail to use

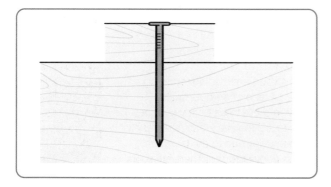

Ideally a nail should be two and a half to three times longer than the thickness of timber it's holding in place, *eg* if fixing a 25mm (1in) piece of wood the nail should be about 75mm (3in) long.

Driving in a nail

Drill a small (2 to 3mm) pilot hole for the nail to make it easier to drive the nail in and, more importantly, to help prevent the wood from splitting. In addition blunt the sharp end of the nail before driving it in – this will also decrease the chance of the wood splitting. To blunt the end, rest the head on something sold and hit the point with a hammer.

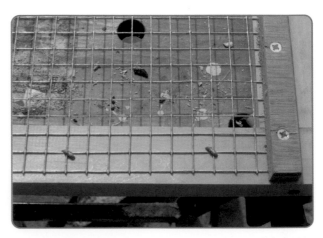

Other fixings

Galvanised wire staples

Staples fired from a gun are a good way of fixing, and are ideal for use with wire or wire mesh, but there are no gun-fired staples available that are rust resistant.

If the staples don't go in straight, drill a 1mm hole for each leg of the staple and drive the staple into these.

Bolts

These now seem to be completely metricated. They are referred to by diameter first and then length, so that a 10mm bolt 75mm long would be referred to as an M10 x 75. The two most usual bolts are coach bolts, which have a domed head, and bolts that have a hexagonal (or square) head.

Spanner size table

Bolt size	Spanner size
M4	7
M5	8
M6	10
M8	13
M10	17
M12	19

Coach bolts are designed to have the head flat against the wood – the square section under the domed head grips in the timber. However, if it doesn't grip it can be difficult to stop the bolt from rotating whilst the nut is being tightened or undone.

Wall plugs

These are plugs driven into a hard surface (such as concrete, brick, or a paving slab) to enable a screw to be fixed into it. They're usually made from plastic. Be careful to get the correct size plug for the size of screw being used, and always use the recommended size masonry bit to drill the hole for the plug. It's a good idea to keep the correct size drill bit in the box with the plugs.

When fitting plugs to secure wood to a masonry base, drill the holes in the wood for the screws, then use a small masonry drill bit through these holes to mark the location of the holes needed in the masonry. Remove the wood and drill the marked holes to the full depth required for the plug.

If a plug is driven into a hole that's too short, or if it needs to be removed for some other reason, drive a screw a little way into the plug and then use a claw hammer to pull the screw and the plug out of the hole.

Frame fixings

Frame (Fischer) fixings have the advantage of being fitted through the wood that's being fixed. Drill the recommended size hole in the wood and use a masonry bit to drill the hole for the plug in the solid base. Drive the frame fixing into the hole and the solid base so that the plastic plug is level with the top of the wood. Drive in the screw supplied with the fixing and tighten it using a screwdriver.

Buy the correct frame fixing for the thickness of timber. This is marked on the plastic plug.

Rawl bolts

These are an adaptation of the wall plugs already described, and provide a very secure fixing.

Pop-rivets

Peel rivets, a type of pop-rivet that peels open before the head pops off, can be used to fix laths of wood together to make a trellis.

Hinges

Flush hinges fit between the door and the frame with no need for a rebate in either. They're not as robust as butt hinges, but are perfectly adequate for lighter doors. They're usually brass-plated and seem to be quite rust resistant.

Butt hinges are the standard type used on doors and require a rebate to be cut in both door and doorframe. Aligning and chopping out the rebates can be a little complex. The hinges are available in steel and brass, and it's the brass variety that should be used outside. Use brass screws with brass hinges.

'T' hinges are available in various lengths from 100mm to 600mm. These are ideal for hanging doors where cutting a rebate isn't possible, *eg* on a ledge door where the edge of the door is only about 25mm thick. They're available galvanised or coated with black japanning. Experience has shown that latter aren't rust resistant, but they can be painted or sprayed to overcome this.

Brackets, spurs and hangers

Brackets are very useful for joints that aren't easy to fix firmly in any other way. Abru Joyner produce a wide range of useful brackets.

Post spurs are ideal for securing fence, gazebo or pergola posts, enabling these to be removed if they should rot. However, they're less likely to rot anyway due to the fact that they're above ground. There are spurs that can be driven into the ground; spurs that can be concreted into place; spurs that can be bolted down onto a flat concrete base; and spurs that can be driven in alongside rotten timber posts to provide a new fixing. Metpost (**www.metpost.co.uk**) provide a wide range of spurs.

Joist hangers do exactly what they say: timber joists can be hung in them. They're fixed to a main support timber or wall and then the ends of a joist or rafter are rested into them. They're ideal for constructing decking.

Concrete and gravel

Gravel is called by different names, and, indeed, consists of different materials, in different parts of the country. If you're unsure what you want, ask your local builders' merchant. Many DIY stores stock gravel in bags, as well as dry mix concrete in bags.

In essence the gravel for concrete is a mix of some form of stone, graded in size from dust to 22mm, often referred to by such terms as '22mm to dust' or '15mm to dust', or sometimes as '15mm all in'. Fine concrete would use '15mm to dust', coarse concrete '22mm to dust'. The ratio of mixes for concrete laid in or under the ground is 4 or 5 gravel to 1 cement, mixed by volume (not weight).

Mix concrete using ordinary cement. Don't use a Masonry cement – this has additives that make it suitable for laying bricks and blocks but not for concrete.

Posts can be set into holes using Postcrete or a similar fast-setting concrete specially formulated for such jobs. Fast-setting concrete is ideal for pads to which bolt-down spurs can be fitted (see **www.hanson.co.uk**).

Catches and door handles

The door handle used on the shed in Chapter 5 is a simple wooden knob with a screw driven into it from the back. One advantage of this type is that any length of screw can be used, enabling the knob to be fixed to any thickness of door.

The handles on the greenhouse door are intended for cupboards but they look as though they'll withstand the weather. These were more complicated to fit because the fixing consists of two bolts, which were too short to go through the door.

To fix these, hold the handle into place on the door and find the best height for it. Use a try square to draw a short line on the door to indicate the location of the handle.

Make a paper template showing the distance between the holes and transfer this to a piece of hardboard.
Hold the template onto the door and drill one hole, the correct size for the bolt. Counterbore (10mm) this hole at the back to a depth that will allow the bolt to protrude far enough to go into the handle.

Push the bolt through the door, fit the template onto it, and use a pencil through the other hole in the template to make a mark that crosses the line drawn previously. Where the lines cross is the location for the other bolt hole. Drill and counterbore this and fix the handle in place.

This will leave two 10mm screw holes on the inside of the door. To cover these, fit the inside handle to a handle plate made from an offcut of TGV cladding or similar thin wood. When the handle has been fitted the plate can be screwed over the holes. Draw a line across the back of the handle plate and use the handle as a guide to mark the location of the two holes in the handle plate. Drill these holes for the bolts, and drive the bolts in to fix the handle to the plate.

The heads of the bolts will fit into the holes and allow the plate to sit flush against the door.

Screw the handle plate to the door using any suitable screws.

Turn buttons

These are a very simple solution to holding a door closed. Try to fix them with a screw that's manufactured from a similar material to the button. The turn button on the shed was fixed with a galvanised slot head screw.

Barrel bolts

Barrel bolts are available in many sizes and some can be padlocked shut. These bolts provide another very straightforward way of keeping a door closed.
Be aware that black japanning on bolts, or any other item, is not weather resistant.

Paints and adhesives

Paints

The only items that have been painted in this book are metal fittings that needed to be rendered a little less obvious or needed to be protected – the timber was treated rather than painted.

Black japanning can be painted over using a metal paint (or metal spray paint) such as Hammerite or Plastikote. When using any paint always undertake a trial run on an area that won't be visible (the underside of a hinge, for instance). This is to ensure that the paint will adhere to the surface and won't adversely affect the basecoat. Follow the manufacturers' instructions carefully, both for safety and application.

When it's time to take a break, wrapping your brush in cling film will stop the paint hardening for an hour or so.

Adhesives

These need to be waterproof and formulated for exterior use. There is a wide range of PVA base adhesives and 'gunnable' types (adhesives that can be used in a mastic gun) to choose from.

When preparing the garage for building some of the structures in this book, the concrete floor was painted using a garage floor paint. The end result certainly made it easier to sweep up at the end of a day's work.

Glass cutting and glazing

Glass cutting

Glass cutting is a confidence trick: the more confidence you have, the more likely you are to succeed.

You'll need a good glass cutter, a straight edge that's not too thick – if it is too thick the cutter will catch on the straight edge; a small jar of white spirit to keep the glass cutter in and to keep it lubricated; a felt-tip pen or chinagraph pencil to mark the glass; a brush to sweep away shards of glass; gloves; and safety glasses. Work on a flat surface spread with an old blanket (to cushion the glass).

Safety When cutting or handling glass, wear gloves that will protect the wrists as well as the hands. Only carry only one sheet of glass at a time. Dispose of the offcuts safely – wrap them in newspaper and mark on it what it contains.

Procedure

Mark the glass by holding it in place and marking the required cut using a felt-tip pen or chinagraph pencil. A mark at each end of the line is adequate – there's no need to draw the whole line.

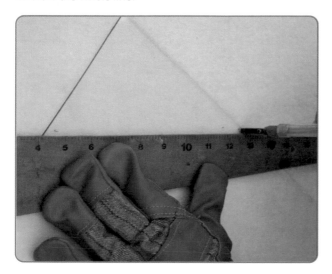

Lay the glass flat and rest the straight edge close to the marks, allowing for the thickness of the glass cutter.

Press firmly down on the glass cutter (don't be afraid, you won't break the glass) and draw the cutter along the straight edge towards you. Try and maintain a steady movement, without stopping. Make sure the cutter goes right to the edge of the glass. You should be able to hear the cutter as it scores the glass. Do *not* go over the score again – once is enough.

Hold the glass on either side and try to snap it along the line of the score. If it doesn't break, lay the score mark over the handle of the cutter and press down on either side. The glass will snap cleanly along the score line.

Brush the blanket off after each cut. *Do not use your hands* – there'll be shards of glass on the blanket.

Corners and extraneous bits of glass can be nibbled off using a pair of pliers. Don't try to remove too much in one go; just nibble away a little at a time.

TIP *You may want to do a few trial runs on a spare piece of glass first, to build up your confidence and to establish the correct distance that needs to be allowed between the straight edge and the marks. If you don't have the confidence to cut the glass, make a template that fits the opening (but not a tight fit) and take it to a local glass supplier who can make the cuts for you.*

Glazing

There are three ways of glazing the greenhouse in Chapter 6: using putty; using acrylic glazing mastic; or using silicon glazing mastic. Wood to which putty is applied must be primed with an oil-based primer to BS 5358 specification or an acrylic primer to BS 5082 specification. Putty cannot be applied over wood stain.

Acrylic glazing mastic is a substitute for putty and is quite easy to use. It's applied from a mastic gun onto the frame.

The glass is pushed onto the mastic.

Additional mastic is applied to the outer surface.

After a suitable time the mastic is smoothed off using a clipt putty knife.

Unfortunately dry weather is required when applying acrylic glazing mastic; both putty and acrylic glazing mastic need to be painted after they've been applied; and both need the glass to be held in place with glazing sprigs (small cut nails).

In addition acrylic glazing mastic can't be used with a cover strip of any kind – it needs to be allowed to breathe.

As a result of all these limitations low modulus silicon glazing mastic was used in the construction of the greenhouse.

This is very sticky, and glass bedded onto it will not be easy to remove. However, it's simple to apply. A thin bead of mastic is applied to the frame.

The glass is bedded into the bead of mastic.

More mastic is applied to the join between the glass and the frame. At this stage the glass will be firmly stuck to the frame.

A cover strip is screwed into place over the join.

Timber types and sizes

Let's review the various types of timber that will be used for the projects set out in this book (for further information visit **www.tonylush.co.uk**).

Sawn timber

Sawn timber sizes are quite straightforward. Lengths are measured in increments of 300mm; the available widths are 100, 115, 125, 150 and 175mm; and it comes in thicknesses of 19, 22, 25, 32, 38, 50, 75 and 100mm. In theory you should be able to buy any combination of these dimensions, but things aren't quite that straightforward since suppliers will usually only stock what they can sell.

Planed timber

Planed square-edge (PSE) timber is usually sold by its nominal size – that is, the size of the sawn timber it was planed from.

Sawn (nominal) size	PSE size
50 x 25mm	44 x 20mm
75 x 25mm	69 x 20mm
100 x 25mm	94 x 20mm
50 x 38mm	44 x 33mm
50 x 50mm	44 x 44mm

Different sizes of sawn and planed timber are both available, but they will be more expensive than the standard sizes.

Cladding

There are many varieties of timber cladding.

Shiplap

This can be one of two types: tongued-and-grooved (T&G) and rebated.

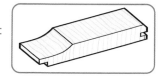

In tongued-and-grooved one edge of the board has a 'tongue' which fits into a groove on the edge of the next board, whereas in rebated shiplap (the type used in this book) one edge

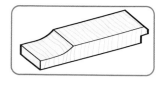

fits into a rebate. The thickness of shiplap boards will vary depending on the timber they were machined from.

Feather-edge

This is a sawn board cut diagonally from a plank of sawn timber. It is referred to by the size of plank it's cut from, *eg* Ex 125 x 25mm feather-edge is cut from a 125 x 25mm sawn plank, giving two planks about 25mm wide at one edge tapering down to about 2mm at the other. It is then pressure treated to make it very durable.

TGV or PMV

These are two names for the same material. The abbreviations stand for 'tongued-and-grooved V-jointed' and 'planed matched V-jointed', the V referring to the chamfer cut on one edge to give a V shape where the planks join.

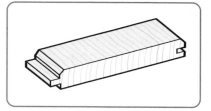

Loglap

Rebated or tongued-and-grooved, this gives a building a pleasing log effect.

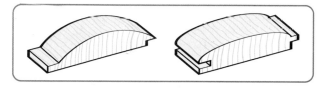

Stripwood

This is the most commonly used name for a plain moulding. It is used extensively in the greenhouse project. It comes in many sizes, and the best way to choose what you want is to look at the racks of mouldings (often made by Richard Burbidge) found in many DIY stores and builders' merchants.

Plywood

Plywood is available in many grades and thicknesses. In places where it will be exposed to all weather conditions it's advisable to use exterior grade or weather and boil proof (WBP) plywood. Differences between grades of plywood are determined by the quality both of the veneers used in their construction and the glue with which they're stuck together.

OSB or oriented strand board is a very robust plywood that will withstand a lot of weathering and is ideal for use in the garden when it is out of sight.

Treated timber

This should be used wherever possible for construction work in the garden, but only in places where it won't come into contact with animals that could chew it. It is available in many of the standard sizes of sawn timber, but local timber mills tend to provide only their own stock sizes. It's therefore best to establish the available sizes of treated timber before designing a structure.

Since the preservative always penetrates the uncut end of treated timber far more deeply than timber treatment applied to a cut end later, whether by soaking or brushing, always try to place uncut ends nearest to any damp conditions.

Roofing battens

These are available as 50 x 25mm (2 x 1in) and 38 x 20mm (1½ x ¾in) in various lengths. They are a good source of treated timber for general use in the garden.

Cutting sheet material using a circular saw

It's essential that the sheet being worked on is well secured and will not fall or move. One way of achieving this is to work on the ground with the sheet propped up on timber.

If an accurate cut is needed you'll need to use a guide of some type, either the one provided with the saw or else a straight edge clamped, nailed, or screwed to the timber or sheet being worked on.

It doesn't matter which side of the saw the guide is fixed for – just measure carefully to ensure that it's set accurately.

It's necessary to support the sheet material well. Rest it on lengths of timber, remembering that cuts made parallel to these supports won't damage them but that transverse cuts will. Therefore lay lengths of thinner, less expensive timber on top of the main supports so that the blade will cut into these sacrificial pieces rather than the larger (more expensive) timbers.

Set the saw blade a few millimetres deeper than the material being cut. This delivers the most efficient cut because the angle at which the saw teeth strike the timber is ideal. In addition, the sacrificial timber may be able to be used again if the cuts are not too deep.

See the section on the pergola in Chapter 4 for details of how to cut lengths of timber. If a lot of timber is to be cut lengthwise it may be worth investing in a table saw.

See the nest box project in Chapter 2 for details of cutting grooves in one side of a sheet of plywood.

Tools

This section deals only with some of the principal tools used to construct the items in this book – it is not intended as an exhaustive list.

Power tools

Chop saw

This is one tool that made the constructions in this book a lot easier. If you have one, or can justify buying one, use

it – it's far more accurate than sawing by hand, whether for 90° cuts or angle cuts. However, before you buy a chop saw check what size timbers it will cut – not only the width of the timber

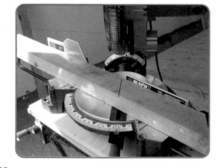

at 90° but also the width it will cut at 45°. The saw used in this book could cut timber just under 125mm wide and up to 75mm deep at 90° but quite a lot less at 45°.

Jigsaw

Jigsaws are very useful – they can be used in areas and to cut shapes that an ordinary saw can't. It helps to have one that has a speed adjustment and a pendulum action. The pendulum action simply means that instead of the saw blade going up and

down like a sewing machine it can be set to work with a slight forward movement to clear the cut.

One advantage of a jigsaw is its ability to accommodate different blades. There are blades for cutting metal, tiles, rubber and, of course, wood and many other materials. When cutting a curve on a thick piece of wood change the blade for a sharp one – it will cut more easily and the blade will tend to twist less. For very intricate cutting fit a profiling blade. This is a lot narrower than a normal blade. For more delicate work fit a blade with more and finer teeth than the normal one. Whenever you have a job to do take a look at the blades available and pick the one that seems best.

Circular saw

These are of considerable use in cutting sheet material and cutting timber along its length. They can also be used for cutting across timber, but a chop saw is easier. The diameter of the blade will determine the maximum depth of cut.

Though the width guide is very useful it's better (space permitting) to fix a straight edge to guide the saw.

Drill/driver

What to call some tools becomes a problem when they can be used for multiple tasks. This is the case, for example, with screwdrivers that are also drills. Cordless drill/drivers, especially the more powerful ones, are as good for drilling a hole as for driving in a screw, and if you haven't got a drill/driver you should buy one. It doesn't need to be very powerful – 7.2v or 12v is OK – but get one with a spare battery. The smaller 7.2v drill/drivers are easier to use for driving in screws because they're lighter, but they're not powerful enough

to drill large holes. Ideally, therefore, you should have two drill/drivers, a large 18 or 24v and a smaller 7.2v, both with a spare battery.

Electric planer

An electric planer can be used for smoothing timber or trimming it to size. If only a small amount of material needs to be removed a planer is better than a saw. The depth of cut is adjustable so that a very aggressive cut or a fine cut can be made. The adjusting knob also has a 'park' position – this is the position the planer must be in when not in use.

Sander

If a coarse belt is used, a belt sander can remove quite large amounts of wood. They're ideal for removing pencil marks and smoothing the ends and cut edges of timber and plywood.

Orbital sanders provide a finer finish where less material needs to be removed. A one-third sheet sander uses standard sheets of abrasive paper cut into three. This means that it's easy to select the grade and type of abrasive paper to use.

Angle grinder

A 110mm mini-angle grinder is another useful multipurpose tool. It can be fitted with discs that will cut metal or stone; a cup-shaped wire brush that will clean

metal, concrete or timber with a very poor surface; or a buffer pad. Buy one with an electronic speed control – it makes delicate work a lot easier.

Hand tools
Clamps

Clamps that work in the same way as a mastic gun are very easy to use, especially as they can be operated with one hand. A piece of wood

should be clamped securely while it's being worked on, sawn, drilled, or sanded. Three or four clamps would seem to be a minimum requirement for many of the tasks in this book.

Corner clamps are very useful when assembling some timber structures.

Sash clamps are used for clamping together larger items such as doors and frames while the glue is setting.

A Heath-Robinson version can be made using timber offcuts and wedges.

If you use a Workmate these have clamps already built in.

Bench

A firm surface to work on is essential. We used two Workmates, which was an ideal solution. But any similar workbench will be fine.

Saws

Universal hard point saws don't need to be sharpened – or rather they can't be sharpened. They're referred to as

universal saws because the teeth are set in such a way that the saw can be used to cut across the grain and along the grain of timber. Most have eight points (teeth) per inch and are 22in (550mm) long. Buy a good one – it makes all the difference.

Chipboard will blunt saws rapidly. When a saw gets too blunt for accurate work on timber, it can be used to cut chipboard, MDF, and other manmade boards.

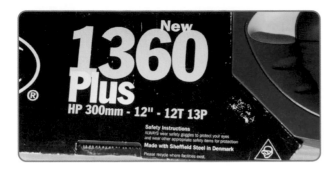

To plug screw holes, use a screw-sink to counterbore the screw hole and a plug-cutter to cut a plug for the hole.

Tenon saws are used for more accurate cutting. They have a hard back (spine) to keep the blade rigid and most are 13in (300mm) long with 13 points per inch.

Hole saws are satisfactory for use on thin sheets of metal or wood but are difficult to use on thicker timber – they tend to bind.

Drill bits
Drill bits for wood can be twist type or flat bits.

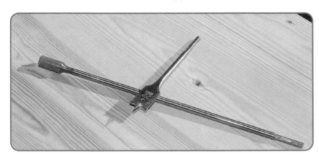

The smallest flat bit is 8mm in diameter, and the largest 35mm. They are designed for use in power drills. Extensions are available that increase their length by 300m to a total of 400mm. Twist drills for wood can also be bought in longer than standard lengths. These longer drills are useful when drilling timber more than 60mm thick. Buy HSS drill bits so that they can be used for metal or wood.

TIP *When drilling damp wood, extract the drill bit every 20mm or so to clear the debris which collects in the twists.*

Countersink bits are available for wood or metal. Don't get into the habit of driving the screw below the surface of the wood with your drill/driver – countersink holes where the head needs to be below the surface.

Masonry drill bits are available in most sizes from 3mm to 10mm and more. They're also available in longer than standard lengths. A long 4mm masonry bit is useful for marking the required location of holes through the holes already drilled in a piece of timber.

Hammers
A claw hammer is essential and a Warrington cross pein hammer is useful for driving in small pins and nails.

Chisels
Chisels are available in a wide range of sizes. They need to be kept sharp by honing with a whetstone. Replace the protection cap after the chisel has been used, since if it's dropped or knocked by a hard object the cutting edge will be damaged. You should always use a wooden mallet with a chisel.

Marking
A try square should be a standard tool that's always to hand when you're woodworking. It's worth getting into the habit of marking a line all the way around any piece of timber that's being cut. This gives you a line to work to.

A combination square can do the same job as a try square but has other uses as well – for instance, it can be set to measure the depth. Be careful not to drop it since this will break the head of the bolt that holds the sliding rule in place.

A sliding bevel is used to set an angle and then to mark it onto another piece of wood.

CREATURE COMFORTS

2

Building a hedgehog summer habitat

There are two types of habitat for a hedgehog: one for shelter during warmer weather and the other for hibernation during the winter. This summer shelter is based on a design from Tiggywinkles, the wildlife hospital organisation (**www.sttiggywinkles.org.uk**).

Procedure

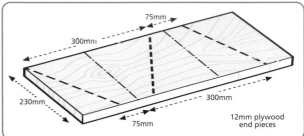

1 Mark the habitat end pieces on a piece of exterior grade plywood – base 300mm, top 75mm, 230mm high. To ensure accuracy, mark the centre line of each end piece and measure from this – there's less chance of the end pieces being skewed if you measure from the middle.

2 Saw along these lines to produce the two end pieces.

Materials

- ■ One 400 x 230mm piece of 12mm exterior grade plywood (thicker would be easier to work with) for end pieces
- ■ One 200mm length of 50 x 25mm roofing batten (or similar timber)
- ■ One 4.7mm length of Ex 125 x 22mm feather-edge cladding
- ■ One 520mm length of 125 x 25mm (5 x 1in) timber, planed or sawn, for top
- ■ 12 1in x 6g screws
- ■ 24 1¼in x 8g screws to fix cladding
- ■ 4 1½in x 8g screws to fix top and end supports
- ■ 50 1in x 8g screws if using screws to fit cladding
- ■ 50 25mm galvanised oval nails to fix cladding
- ■ Timber treatment

Tools

- ■ Universal hard point saw
- ■ Jigsaw
- ■ Extension lead
- ■ RCD (or safety plug)
- ■ Drill/driver
- ■ Twist drill bits:
  - 10mm
  - 5mm
  - 4mm
  - 2mm
- ■ Countersink
- ■ Screwdriver bits
- ■ Posi (PZ) No 2
- ■ Hammer
- ■ Nail punch
- ■ Workbench
- ■ Clamp
- ■ Try square
- ■ Pencil
- ■ Tape measure
- ■ Safety glasses
- ■ Dust mask
- ■ Ear defenders
- ■ Gloves

3 Screw a short length of 50 x 25mm batten to the top of both end pieces and saw the excess batten off flush with the sides. These battens are for screwing the top to.

4 Cut six 300mm pieces of Ex 125 x 22mm feather-edge to clad the end pieces (three for each). At the bottom of one plywood end piece (on the opposite side to the batten) nail one 300mm length of feather-edge, taking care to align the thick edge with the base of the end piece. Use galvanised 25mm ovals to fix the top (the thin section) and the bottom of the feather-edge. Drilling 2mm holes for the nails should prevent the feather-edge from splitting. If the nails you use are too long bend (clench)

them over on the inside – this will improve their grip.

If you prefer you can use 1in x 6g screws to fix the feather-edge. Drill 4mm clearance holes for these.

5 Evenly space the other two lengths of feather-edge so that they overlap each other leaving an exposed area of about 60mm (this will vary with the width of the boards). Nail or screw them in place. Blunt the

sharp end of the nails prior to use – this will help to stop them splitting the wood. Clad the second end piece in exactly the same way.

6 When the feather-edged boards have been securely nailed to the plywood ends, saw off the excess flush with the plywood.

Safety Clamp the **work in place to hold it firm while sawing the feather-edge.**

7 Mark the entrance opening, 150mm high x 100mm wide, on one end piece. Use a jigsaw to cut out the opening. Drill a 10mm hole in each of the top corners to start with: these will allow the jigsaw blade to turn when it reaches them.

8 Cut six 520mm lengths of feather-edge to form the sides of the habitat (three lengths for each side).

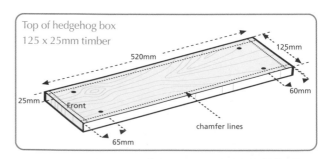

Top of hedgehog box
125 x 25mm timber

520mm · 125mm · 25mm · Front · 60mm · chamfer lines · 65mm

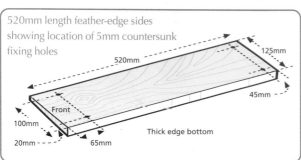

520mm length feather-edge sides showing location of 5mm countersunk fixing holes

520mm · 125mm · 45mm · Front · 100mm · Thick edge bottom · 20mm · 65mm

9 Draw a line on the front end of each feather-edge plank, 65mm from the end. This will provide a small overlap at the front of the box. Draw a second line 45mm from the other end (the back). Make marks on these lines 20mm and 100mm up from the thick edge of the board. These marks indicate the location of the screw holes needed to fix the feather-edge to the end pieces. Drill and countersink these holes using a 5mm drill bit.

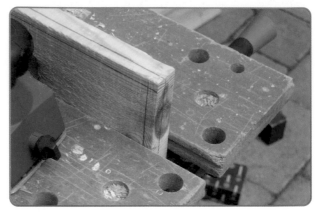

11 Cut a 520mm length of 125 x 25mm timber to act as the top. Chamfer off the edges to allow water to run off easily (make a line to mark the chamfer and plane to that line).

Use 1½in screws to attach the top to the battens fixed to the end pieces. The location for the countersunk 5mm holes can be established by careful measurement. On the hedgehog home these were 25mm in from the edges, 65mm from the front, and 60mm from the back.

Treat the habitat with a suitable non-toxic timber preservative (see Chapter 1 for choice of timber treatments). Allow this to dry and then entice your hedgehog in to enjoy his new surroundings!

10 Use 1¼in screws to attach the two bottom pieces of feather-edge to both end pieces, making sure the screws go directly into the edge of the plywood end piece. Screw the other 520mm lengths into place, leaving 60mm of exposed overlap to match the feather-edge on the end pieces. Saw or plane off any feather-edge that protrudes above the top of the plywood end pieces.

Building an insect hibernacula

Many gardens are kept unnecessarily tidy and consequently provide few hibernation opportunities for insect life. Most insects benefit the garden in one way or another, so why not provide an over-wintering place for them? In this section we show how to make a simple hibernation place (hibernacula) for insects – the insect hibernation boxes in your local garden centre will provide you with further ideas and inspiration.

Procedure

1 Cut a 425mm length of 150 x 25mm timber to form the back and front of the hibernacula. Mark the centre of the plank at each end and join the marks to form a centre line along the length of the timber. This can be done using a combination square set to half the width of the plank (75mm). Using the combination square from both sides will indicate if the mark is central.

2 Mark the apex on both ends of the plank so that the apex corner (the top corner) is 90°. This can be done using the 45° guide on a combination square.

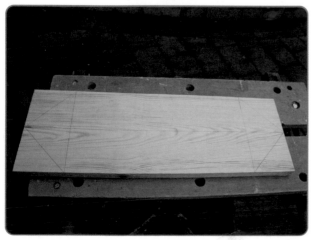

Materials
- 510mm 150 x 25mm sawn timber, untreated, for main carcass
- 5–10 bamboos about 1.5m long
- 4 2in x 8g screws
- 300mm Ex 125 x 25mm feather-edge or similar for the roof
- 8 25mm galvanised clout nails
- 2 screw eyes
- String
- UHU glue

Tools
- Universal hard point saw
- Jigsaw
- Extension lead
- RCD (or safety plug)
- Belt sander may be needed
- Drill/driver
- Twist drill bits:
  8mm
  5mm
  2mm
- Flat drill bits:
  20mm flat
- Screwdriver bits: Posi (PZ) No 2
- Hammer
- Workbench
- Clamps
- Try square
- Combination square
- Pencil
- Tape measure
- Drill carrier to act as a guide for hole sizes
- Safety glasses
- Dust mask
- Ear defenders
- Gloves

3 Cut the apexes marked at either end of the plank. Mark a line across the middle of the plank equidistant from each apex. Do not cut the plank in half yet.

5 Securely clamp the plank to a bench or workbench. Drill a 20mm hole inside the circle near its circumference. This is to allow the jigsaw blade to enter.

4 Draw round a suitably sized paint tin (100mm in diameter) to mark a circle on the centre line of the plank. This circle should touch the base of the triangle forming the apex.

6 Use a jigsaw to cut out the circle on one end of the plank only. Don't push the saw too hard – work slowly and concentrate on following the line.

TIP *Have the jigsaw set at maximum or near maximum speed and on full pendulum setting, and make sure the blade is sharp (fit a new one).*

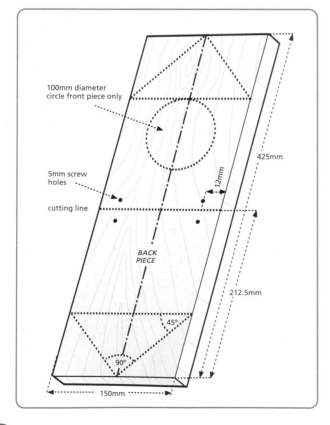

100mm diameter circle front piece only

5mm screw holes

cutting line

12mm

425mm

212.5mm

45°

90°

150mm

BACK PIECE

7 Cut along the centre line marked in Step 3 to form two end pieces. A chop saw is ideal for this but a universal hard point saw will do the job. Lay the end with the hole in it (the front) on top of the other end piece. If necessary, cut them so that they're the same length. Use a pencil to mark the 100mm hole on the second end piece.

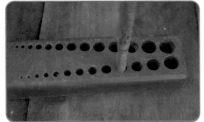

8 Drill a series of holes around the pencilled circle on the back piece of the hibernacula. The drill bit needs to be the correct size for the ends of the bamboo canes to fit into its holes, so either drill a few trial holes to find the best size or try fitting the canes in the drill carrier. They don't have to be a tight fit. An 8mm bit was used for the hibernacula in this project. Don't drill all the way through the back piece.

TIP *If your drill has one, fit its depth gauge rod to ensure that the bit goes a set depth into the wood. Alternatively, wrap a length of masking tape around the drill bit to give you an idea how far it's gone in.*

9 Drill two 5mm screw holes at the bottom of the front and back pieces. These are 10mm up from the bottom and 30mm in from the edges. Cut the 70mm long 150 x

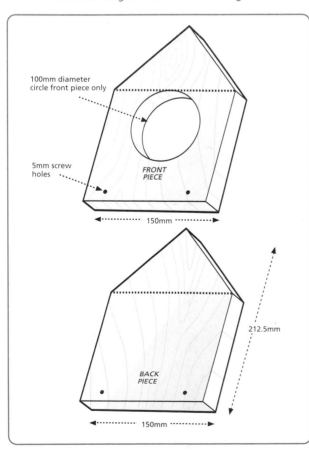

100mm diameter circle front piece only

5mm screw holes

FRONT PIECE

150mm

BACK PIECE

150mm

212.5mm

25mm base piece. Ensuring that you align the base accurately on to the front or back piece, clamp it and use 2in x 8g screws to screw one end piece to the base. Then screw the other end piece to the base. Drilling 2mm pilot holes for the screws in the end of the base will help to stop the wood splitting, as will driving the screws in slowly.

10 Cut short lengths of bamboo so that when they're pushed into the 8mm holes in the back they're flush with the outside face of the front end. You may find it easier to cut the bamboo quite long, push it into the 8mm hole, and then mark where your accurate cut needs to be, then remove the bamboo and cut it to length. Remove the front end piece with the large hole in it.

Safety If using a chop saw to cut the bamboo, always cut long lengths – don't try to hold a short length close to the blade! Leftover bits can be used in the garden.

11 Having cut enough lengths of bamboo to fit into all the 8mm holes, push them into the holes – a gentle tap with a hammer will ensure they're fully in. If they won't stay in the holes glue them in place with UHU or a similar adhesive.

12 Replace the end piece so that all the bamboos are collected in the hole.

13 Measure the length from the inside face of the back piece to the outside face of the front and cut bamboos to this length. Rest these in the large hole. Keep cutting and fitting bamboos until the large hole is full. Hammer a few more in to wedge the canes tightly in place.

14 If you see the need, clamp the hibernacula securely in your workbench and use a belt sander to level off the canes at the front – but the insects won't care about them being uneven!

15 To form the roof, cut two 150mm lengths of Ex 125 x 25mm feather-edge and use 30mm galvanised clout nails to fix them to the apex of the end pieces. The feather-edge needs to overlap at the front and sides to keep rain off the insects. As usual, drilling a 2mm pilot hole for the nails will help to stop the feather-edge splitting.

16 Screw two screw eyes through the roof cladding into the top of the end pieces. Tie string through these to hang the hibernacula.

Building a kennel

It's important that a kennel is used with the best interests of the dog in mind – not just as a means of keeping your pet out of the house and out of your way. Dogs are social animals and need company, and should be allowed to run free, so a kennel is intended purely as a temporary shelter.

A kennel should be waterproof and draught-proof, located in a cool area, and situated so that the dog can look out while sitting in the dry and/or shade. While the dog is using it, the kennel must not get hot in the summer or cold in the winter. It should be at least big enough for the dog to lie at full stretch, turn around, and sit up.

As well as building a kennel, consider how to prepare the garden for your dog. Most dogs like a sand pit and many will enjoy drinking from, and playing with, a water feature. However, take care to avoid deep ponds and sharp edges.

Materials

- The amount of material you require will depend on the size of kennel you want to build. For the kennel described here, the following materials were needed:
- 10m of 50 x 25mm PSE for the main structure legs, floor supports, and roof supports
- 3.2m of 100 x 25mm PSE for the bargeboard
- 2m of 75 x 25mm PSE for the fascia
- 30m of shiplap cladding
- Small box (100) of 1½in x 8g screws
- Small box (100) of 1¼in x 8g screws
- Exterior adhesive
- 2440 x 1220mm sheet of 12mm exterior grade plywood for the floor and roof
- 4.2m of 38 x 18mm treated batten to provide roof spacing for the insulation
- 2 1200 x 450mm sheets of 25mm polystyrene for insulation
- 1.5m of 1m wide under-slating felt
- 40 30mm and 40 40mm galvanised oval nails to secure the roof and shiplap cladding
- 1m of 25 x 25mm wooden angle moulding for the apex
- Timber treatment or stain

Tools

- Universal hard point saw
- Tenon saw
- Chop saw
- Jigsaw
- Extension lead
- RCD (or safety plug)
- Belt sander
- Drill/driver
- Twist drill bits:
  8mm
  5mm
  2mm
- Plug cutter and screw-sink if screw holes are going to be plugged
- Countersink
- Screwdriver bits: Posi (PZ) No 2
- Hammer
- Workbench
- Sash clamps
- Smaller clamps
- Try square
- Combination square
- Pencil
- Tape measure
- Sliding bevel
- Safety glasses
- Dust mask
- Ear defenders
- Gloves

Kennel sizes

Breed of dog	Outside measurements (mm)		Overall
	Width	Height	height (mm)
Terrier	610	640	770
Labrador	760	940	980
German Shepherd	910	1080	1200
Great Dane	1080	1240	1380

The kennel built in this chapter is for a small Labrador (see photograph).

Procedure

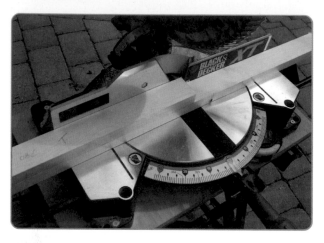

3 Mark the first 5mm screw hole 50mm from one end, and then the other holes at about 260mm, 460mm and 660mm. Drill the holes using a 5mm bit and countersink` them.

1 The corner posts are constructed using eight 780mm lengths of 50 x 25mm PSE timber, screwed and glued together to form four L-shaped posts. The length of these posts depends on the height of the kennel.

2 Mark the required screw holes on the 50mm face of four of the 780mm lengths of 50 x 25mm PSE. The holes need to be 10mm in from one edge so that the screws are driven into the centre of the edge of the adjoining timber.

TIP *This can be achieved by setting a combination square so that it's exactly half the width of the timber (10mm) and then using it to mark the holes.*

TIP *If you clamp the four lengths together the holes can be drilled in all of them at the same time.*

4 For each corner post, apply exterior grade adhesive to the 25mm face of one of the undrilled 780mm lengths, clamp it and one of the

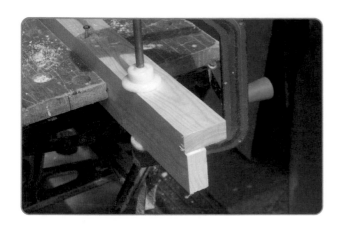

drilled lengths together, and screw them using 1½in x 8g screws. Be sure that the pieces of 50 x 25mm line up at the edges and ends.

TIP *Drill pilot holes into the 25mm edge using a 2mm bit.*

5 Stand the corner posts upright and arrange them so that they're all facing the correct way, then mark the bottom of each so that they can be relocated correctly. It's very important to get the 'L' shapes the correct way around, or the shiplap won't fit (see Step 9).

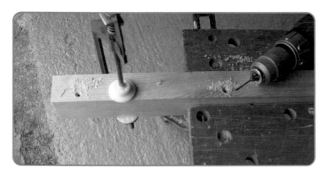

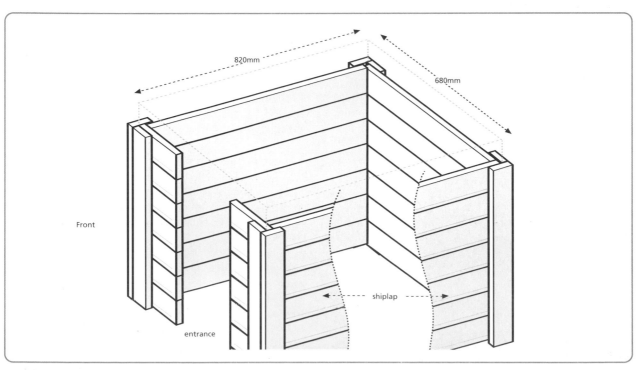

820mm

680mm

Front

shiplap

entrance

6 Next we build the sides. For this kennel you'll need to cut twelve 820mm lengths of shiplap for the two sides, but the number and length will vary depending on the actual size of kennel you want to build.

7 Cut eight 680mm lengths of shiplap for one end and as temporary bracing (see Steps 12 and 13) – again, their actual length will depend on the size of the kennel.

8 Arrange some form of bench so that the sides can be laid flat while they're being built (two workbenches would be ideal).

9 The first plank of shiplap starts 80mm up from the bottom of the corner posts – this raises the kennel off the ground and allows for the floor support to be added later. To ensure this is done accurately, set a combination square to 80mm and mark a line on the inside of each corner post. Also, take care that the corner posts are the correct way round – the shiplap should be fixed to the 25mm face of the L-shaped post. If it isn't, there'll be no room to fix the shiplap to the inner section of the 'L'. Use a try square or combination square to ensure the shiplap is square to the posts.

10 Lay two 820mm lengths of shiplap onto the 25mm face of the corner posts so that one is at the top and the other at the bottom. This will hold the corner posts parallel. Use sash clamps to hold the corner posts firmly onto the shiplap. Clamp the bottom length of shiplap to the 25mm face of the corner posts so that it's touching the 80mm line. Drill and countersink 5mm clearance holes for the 1½ in screws, and then drill 2mm pilot holes into the corner posts. Locate the screw holes in the shiplap carefully so that the screws go through the thick section and not the moulded area (the screw may show if it does). Screw the shiplap at both ends.

11 Fix the remaining lengths of shiplap to complete one side, taking care to ensure that the tongues are pushed into the rebates. One screw per plank should be sufficient. Construct the other side in the same way, taking care to

screw the shiplap to the 25mm inner face and to align it with the 80mm mark.

> **TIP** *If all the lengths of shiplap are cut with square ends and the same length the frame should be square, but as each length is added check it using a try square. If necessary pull it into shape as each length of shiplap is added.*

12 Use four of the eight 680mm lengths of shiplap, screwed to the top and bottom of each corner post, to

temporarily hold the sides together. The bottom ones must align with the 80mm pencil mark.

13 Including the two bracing lengths, screw six of your 680mm shiplap planks to the back of the kennel (*ie* the end without an entrance). It may be necessary to realign the top temporarily located length of shiplap. Take care that these planks align with the pieces of shiplap already fixed to the kennel sides.

Stand the kennel on a flat base and check the distance at the top between its diagonally opposite corner pieces. If they're the same, the kennel is square; if they're not, push the kennel into shape until they are.

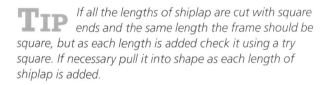

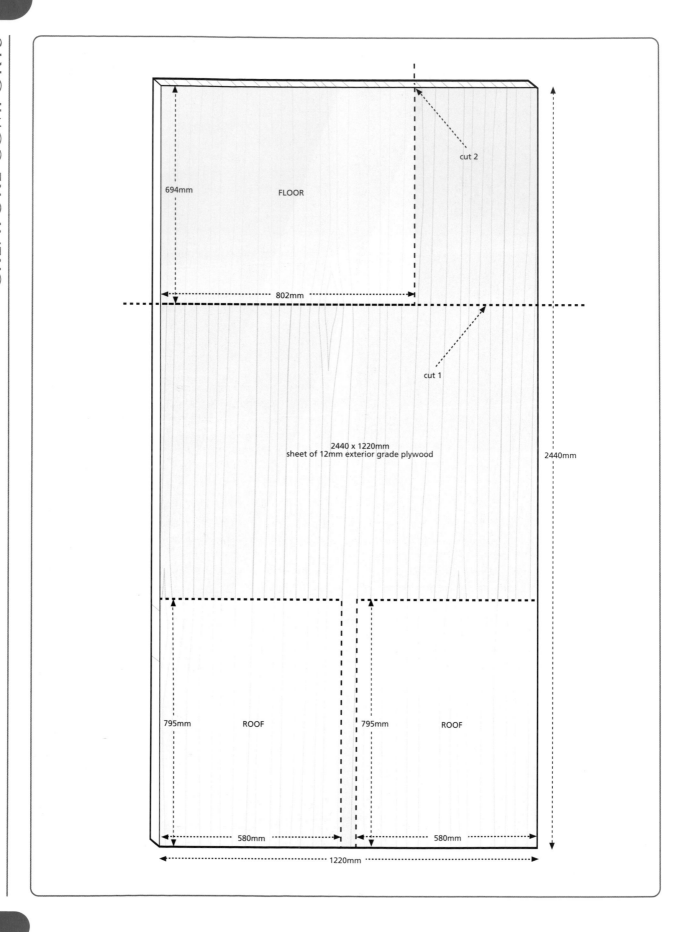

cut 2

694mm

FLOOR

802mm

cut 1

2440 x 1220mm
sheet of 12mm exterior grade plywood

2440mm

795mm   ROOF   795mm   ROOF

580mm   580mm

1220mm

Fitting the floor

The floor is cut from a sheet of 12mm exterior grade plywood and is fitted from underneath, held in place with 25 x 50mm PSE support battens. These are screwed to the L-shaped corner posts. The floor can be removed for cleaning by simply removing the support battens.

1 Stand the kennel on one end and measure into the grooves of the shiplap to establish the correct size for the floor.

TIP *To ensure the floor will be the correct size, cut two battens that fit exactly into the grooves of the bottom section of shiplap, one the length of the kennel and the other its width. Use these to mark out the floor. Ask the supplier of the plywood if they'll cut it to size but don't have the roof sheets cut yet. For details of how to cut large sheet material see chapter 1.*

2 Cut the floor section from the sheet, taking care to get the corners square. Do not cut the roof panels yet. Check that the floor fits. If the cuts are accurate the floor will help to pull the kennel into shape. Don't fix the floor – it's intended to be removable.

3 Cut two 820mm lengths of 50 x 25mm PSE for the edge floor supports and two 690mm lengths for the end floor supports. Drill and countersink 5mm holes in the ends of each support, taking care that the screws will go into the corner posts.

4 With the floor in place, use 1½in x 8g screws to screw the floor supports to the corner posts so that they're tight against the floor. At this stage you can either leave the floor in place or remove it to make the kennel lighter to handle. If you remove it, label the support pieces so that they go back in the same places when you put the floor back.

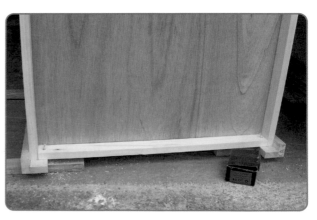

Rafter 'A' frames and gusset plates

1 Clamp a piece of 50 x 25mm PSE (about 1100mm long) to the inside of the shiplap on the back of the kennel. It must be in the centre of the back and vertical. This forms a temporary support for the apex of the roof. (If the kennel isn't on a level base,

the temporary support must rest on a centreline drawn on the inside of the back shiplap.) Clamp one length of 50 x 25mm PSE (rafter) to this vertical support so that it's resting on the side shiplap. Move the timbers up and down the upright support to achieve the roof pitch that looks best.

2 Our kennel has a roof with a 35° pitch. If you're going to use this pitch set your chop saw to 35° and cut one end of a piece of 50 x 25mm PSE. If you're not using a chop saw, set a sliding bevel to the angle of the cut while the rafter is still clamped in place and cut one end of the rafter to this angle.

3 Rest the cut end of the rafter onto the inside face of the shiplap, close to the corner post.

4 Clamp the other end of the rafter to the temporary upright. Mark its position at the centre of the upright, and using this mark as a guide cut the top of the rafter to an angle of 35° (or your preferred angle). This is the first of four rafters.

TIP *Make a pencil line on the rafter to show the general direction of the cut – it's all too easy to cut at the wrong angle.*

5 Use the first rafter as a template to cut another. Rest the two rafters in place. Their tops should meet at the centre of the temporary support and the feet should rest on or near the top of the shiplap. Trim them if they don't fit properly,

remembering that when trimming two angles to fit you should always trim a little off both angles – not a lot off one.

When the rafters are a good fit, use one of them as a template for the two rafters for the front. Cut the front rafters and remove the temporary upright.

6 Lay the two rafters on an offcut from the main sheet of plywood so that they meet perfectly. Mark around the apex to give you the cutting lines for the gusset plate.

7 Cut out the gusset plate. Before you fix it, use it as a template to mark out the other gusset plate for the front.

inward. Drill and countersink the hole near the end of the 'A' frame so that the screw doesn't go through the moulded section of the shiplap. These screws will go through the length of shiplap that's there just to hold the sides together (this can be removed later). Screw the back 'A' frame the same way.

8 Screw and glue the gusset plate into place, taking care that the rafters stay together at the apex. Make up the other 'A' frame in the same way. When the glue has set, check that both 'A' frames still fit.

9 Use 1½in screws through the rafter and into the shiplap to secure the front 'A' frame in place, with the gusset facing

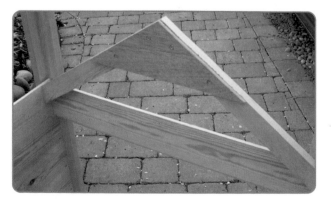

10 Use the 'A' frame to guide the saw while you cut the posts to the correct angle.

11 Tidy the cut end if necessary. A belt sander would be ideal for this.

Boarding the back apex

1 Cut a shiplap board the same length as the end pieces (684mm) and push it into place so that the groove fits over the tongue. It will probably be necessary to loosen the screws holding the 'A' frame in place in order to achieve this.

Cut another length of shiplap so that it rests over the tongue of the one just fitted. Cut a third piece if necessary. Mark these along the top of the 'A' frame. Remove them and cut along the marks.

The front apex will be cut later.

2 Put the cut lengths back into place, check they fit (they shouldn't protrude above the 'A' frame), and trim them if necessary. When they do fit, screw through the 50 x 25mm PSE of the 'A' frame into the shiplap using 1½in screws. It may be necessary to glue the small triangle of shiplap at the top. Tighten up any loosened screws.

The roof and the front

1 Check that the dog can lie down inside the kennel.

2 Before the front gable can be clad, you need to establish the size of the opening. Remove the bottom length of shiplap that held the front together and, unless you know what sort of gap your dog can easily walk through, cut a large square of cardboard and fix it to the remaining (upper) length of shiplap. Cut an opening in this that seems about the right size and encourage your dog to walk through it, turn around, and lie in the kennel. This will give you a better idea of what size the opening needs to be. Adjust the size of the hole in the cardboard until you've got it exactly right. Then remove the cardboard and use it later to establish the length of the shiplap side pieces you'll need to form the opening (for our kennel this was

200mm). Replace the bottom length of shiplap if the kennel seems unstable.

3 Before the front is clad it's easier to cut and make the initial fit for the roof panels. Decide on the size of roof you need, allowing an overlap at the front and enough overlap at the sides for rainwater to drop to the ground rather than onto the kennel (our kennel roof needed two pieces 600 x 1200mm). Cut the plywood to the required size or get it cut at the store you bought it from.

    The back of the roof is flush with the L-shaped corner pieces, the front has an overlap of 120mm, and the sides overlap by 120mm. These overlaps are optional but recommended.

    If the sheets are to overlap at the ridge one side will need to be 12mm wider to allow for this.

4 Lay the pieces of ply in place so that they touch or overlap at the ridge.

5 Carefully measure to establish the locations of the 'A' frames and drill and countersink 5mm holes in the roof plywood to coincide with them. (Ensure that the 'A' frames are upright by clamping them to the roof plywood.)

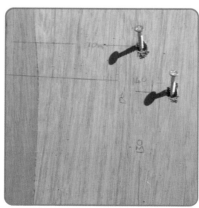

Screw the plywood into place using 1½in x 8g screws. The screws that go into the top of the corner posts need to be vertical so that they go into the end grain, whereas the screws that go into the 'A' frame can be at right angles to the plywood.

    The roof plywood can now be removed to allow the front shiplap to be fitted.

6 Cut ten 200mm pieces of shiplap to the required length for the front (five for each side of the opening).

    Before removing the top temporary length of shiplap to replace it with the new short side pieces, fit sash clamps to hold the kennel together at the front. Screw the side pieces to the L-shaped corner posts using 1½in x 8g screws.

    When all the side pieces of shiplap have been screwed into place to give the correct height opening, refit and screw the top length of shiplap back into place (to do this it will be necessary to loosen the 'A' frame). Note that the topmost piece of shiplap may need to be glued – use a clamp to hold it until the glue is dry.

    When the full-length piece of shiplap has been replaced it will hold the sides together and the sash clamps can be removed.

    Clad the apex above the opening in the same way as the back was done.

TIP *Where the screws go through the gusset plate and into the shiplap you may find 1½in screws too short and 2in too long. To overcome this, drill a shallow 8mm hole in the gusset plate to allow the 1½in screws to go in further and bite into the shiplap.*

7 The side pieces for the opening are supported by a length of 50 x 25mm PSE with an angle cut at the top to fit against the rafters of the front apex. This angle will be the same as for the roof (35°). Cut two of these lengths, one for each side of the opening. If you're using a chop saw, cut the uprights a little longer than needed

and then trim small amounts off the base until they fit exactly to the edge of the side pieces.

Drill and countersink 5mm holes in the uprights (one hole for each section of shiplap) and, using 1½in x 8g screws, screw them to the shiplap.

Sand the ends of the shiplap around the entrance until they're smooth.

TIP *It's not ideal to screw the side pieces to the floor because the latter needs to be easy to remove. However, if you feel the side pieces will be damaged by the dog going in and out use two L-shaped metal brackets to secure them to the floor.*

8 Decide on the type of roofing for the kennel. There are many alternatives, including roofing felt, cedar shingles (both described in Chapter 5), and self-adhesive flashing (described in the section on building a rabbit hutch later in this chapter). Here we provide details of how to construct an insulated shiplap roof.

9 Refit the sheets of 12mm plywood you cut earlier, taking care that the screws go back into the holes made in Step 5. This will ensure that the 'A' frames are upright.

Fix 38 x 18mm treated roofing batten, on edge, to the roof. The upper ends of the battens at the front and back need to be cut at a 35° angle so that they meet at the apex, and their feet need to be cut at the same angle to form a vertical surface to which the fascia can be fitted.

When the battens have been cut to length, drill and countersink four 5mm holes, 6mm in from the edge of the roofing plywood at the front and back. Clamp the battens into place and screw 1¼in x 8g screws up through the 12mm plywood roofing into the batten.

10 The centre battens can overlap at the apex, where they should be screwed together using a 1½in x 8g screw.

Take care to get the ends of the battens flush with the edge of the roofing (this can be achieved by laying the central battens on the roof and marking the angle at which they need to be cut at the apex). Make sure that the angle is cut in the right direction.

11 Cut the sheets of 25mm polystyrene insulation to fit between the battens (using a saw is probably the most accurate way to cut these).

12 Cut lengths of under-slating felt to rest on top of the insulation. This can be stapled or nailed in place.

13 Cut 12 lengths of shiplap exactly the same length as the roof plywood. Clamp the first two lengths into place at the bottom edges of the roof, allowing sufficient overlap to cover the fascia when it's fitted. Then lay the other five planks on each side, overlapping downwards. If necessary adjust the overlap at the fascia until the planks meet or nearly meet at the ridge.

14 Nail the shiplap into place, using 30mm galvanised ovals at the thin edge and 40mm ovals in the thicker section. Drill 2mm holes in the shiplap to prevent the nails from splitting it.

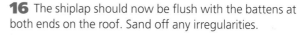

15 To enable the bargeboards to fit, mark the ends of the shiplap roofing planks and saw them off flush to the battens, using a tenon saw.

16 The shiplap should now be flush with the battens at both ends on the roof. Sand off any irregularities.

Bargeboard and fascia

To make the bargeboards, first cut a single piece of 100 x 25mm PSE, about 40mm longer than is necessary. Screw this into place, aligning it with the shiplap on the roof. Use a spirit level to mark a vertical line to the required angle at the apex (see 'Building a Shed' in Chapter 5 for more details of how to mark the angle on the bargeboard).

1 Remove the bargeboard and cut the angle indicated by the vertical line. Cut the same angle on another length of PSE to provide the other half of the bargeboard. Hold them in position to check that the angles are correct, and then screw them into place.

2 Use a spirit level to mark the vertical on the bottom edge or foot of the bargeboard.

3 Use a spirit level to mark a horizontal line on the foot of the rafter that coincides with the vertical line.

Repeat the entire process to make and fit the bargeboards at the other end of the kennel. All four bargeboards can then be screwed in place using 1½in x 8g screws into the roof battens.

The fascia is made from 75 x 25mm PSE and is cut to length so that it fits into place between the two bargeboards at either end. It is screwed to the feet of the roofing battens. (For further details of fitting bargeboards and fascia, see Chapter 5.)

If the fascia is cut a millimetre longer than necessary it can be squeezed into place by loosening the screws that fix the bargeboard just enough to allow the fascia to fit, and then tightening the screws again to hold it in place.

4 Use a good external adhesive to fix a length of angle moulding along the apex of the roof to cover the join between the topmost shiplap planks.

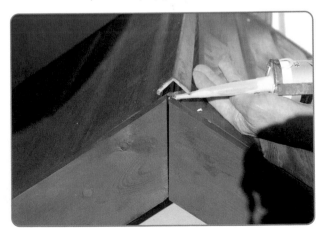

Filling screw holes

The holes for the screws can be hidden using either filler or wooden plugs.

1 To plug the screw holes use a screw-sink to open up the top of the screw hole and a plug-cutter to cut the plug (see Chapter 1).

2 Cut enough plugs for the bargeboards (four in this case) from a piece of timber similar to that actually used.

3 Removing one screw at a time, drill a hole using the drill bit section of the tool. This will drill the correct size hole for the plug. Drive the screw back into the hole, making sure the head goes fully in.

4 Use a screwdriver to prise the plug out of the timber when it's needed.

5 Apply glue to the plug and tap it into the hole.

6 Allow the glue to dry before chiselling off the plug. Start by positioning the chisel so that it cuts off about half the length of the plug.

7 Chisel off the rest of the plug close to the bargeboard. Then sand the plug head down and stain it the same colour as the rest of the timber.

Finally, paint or stain the kennel in the colour of your choice. Our kennel was painted with Sadolin Super Deck Jungle Green, while the roof was treated with Cuprinol Garden Wood Preservative Autumn Brown

Building a nesting box

These instructions cover how to make a nesting box with an entry hole, an open-fronted box, and a bat box. Whether these have a removable roof or not, the basic structure is the same for each design.

Start by deciding if the roof is to lift off. If it does, you'll be able to look at the birds in their nest (if you can reach the box easily) and cleaning it will be simpler. If the roof doesn't lift off, the base will have to be unscrewed when the box needs cleaning.

Boxes for tits, sparrows or starlings should be fixed 2–4m up a tree or on a wall and facing between north and east, to avoid strong sunlight and the wettest winds. The birds need a clear flight path to the nest without any clutter directly in front of the entrance.

Open-fronted boxes for robins and wrens need to be below 2m and well hidden in vegetation.

As regards dimensions, the size of the entrance hole and the structure will influence the types of bird that use the box. If the entrance hole is too large it will let in squirrels and predators like magpies. See Steps 18–19 below.

By putting up different types of box, several species may be attracted. Many birds enter nesting boxes during the autumn and winter, looking for a suitable place to roost or perhaps to feed, so try to get them fixed in the autumn.

Finally, before you even start to build a nesting box you need to decide how it's to be fixed in place. A box with a removable roof can be hung by making a hole in the back apex while the roof is off and then driving a screw or nail through the hole. A box with a fixed roof can be hung by

fixing a bracket to the back.

However, nailing or screwing the box to a tree may damage the tree, so it might be preferable to attach it either with string that won't rot, wire, or some form of strap around the trunk or a branch. If it's to be held in place with straps you'll need to cut rebates in the side pieces during construction, as described in the section on making a curved-roof nesting box.

If you decide to use wire, holes can be drilled in the side for this prior to fitting the base. It is also advisable to thread a length of hosepipe onto the wire to prevent it damaging the tree. Remember that trees grow in girth as well as height, so check the strap or wire every two to three years and loosen it if necessary.

Materials
- ■ 1.3m of 150 x 20mm gravel board for main body
- ■ 460mm of Ex 150 x 25mm feather-edge for roof
- ■ 2 2in x 10g dowel screws (for removable roof only)
- ■ 16 2in x 8g screws
- ■ 8 1½in x 8g screws
- ■ 8 1in x 8g screws for the roof
- ■ Small packet of 30mm galvanised clout nails for nailing roof into place
- ■ 25mm side hook and eye (for removable roof only)

Tools
- ■ Universal hard point saw
- ■ Tenon saw
- ■ Chop saw
- ■ Belt sander
- ■ Jigsaw
- ■ Extension lead
- ■ RCD (or safety plug)
- ■ Drill/driver
- ■ Twist drill bits
  - 10mm
  - 6mm
  - 4mm
  - 5mm
  - 2mm
- ■ Countersink
- ■ Flat drill bits
  - 32mm (for house sparrows, nuthatches and lesser spotted woodpeckers)
  - 28mm (for great tits, tree sparrows and pied flycatchers)
  - 25mm (for blue, coal and marsh tits)
  - 16mm (for bat box)
- ■ Screwdriver bits Posi (PZ) No 2
- ■ Hammer
- ■ Workbench
- ■ Clamps
- ■ Try square
- ■ Combination square
- ■ Pencil
- ■ Tape measure
- ■ Sliding bevel
- ■ Safety glasses
- ■ Dust mask
- ■ Ear defenders
- ■ Gloves

Building a nesting box with a removable roof

1 Using a try square, make a mark 460mm from one end of your piece of 150 x 25mm gravel board. This length will form both the back (260mm) and front (190mm) of the nesting box. Cut the back piece from this, to a length of 260mm from apex to base. This will leave a little more than is needed to form the 190mm front.

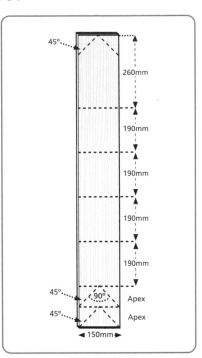

TIP *If the chop saw blade doesn't cut through the full depth of the timber, use a universal hard point saw to finish the cut.*

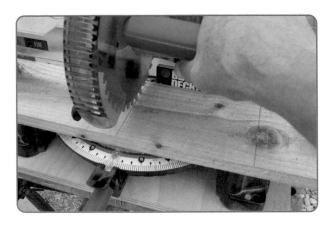

2 Cut another length of board 600mm long to form the sides and the base. Mark a line 190mm from one end and cut to this line; mark another line 190mm further along the board and cut to this; and finally cut the remaining piece of timber to 190mm. The purpose of marking and cutting each line individually is to allow for the thickness of the saw blade.

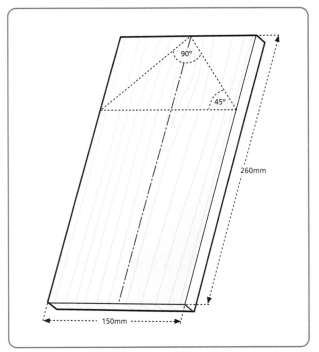

3 Mark the centre, 75mm in from each edge, on the 260mm length of board forming the back of the box. Use a combination square to check the line is correct.

4 Using a combination square, mark the 45° angles that form the apex of the roof. Alternatively use a chop saw set to 45° to cut the angle.

5 Cut along the 45° lines to form the apex of the box, with a chop saw if it is big enough, otherwise with a universal saw. Even if the chop saw doesn't go all the way through the timber it will do a lot of the work very accurately. The remainder of the cut can then be done using a universal saw. It will certainly promote accuracy if you start with the chop saw before cutting the rest by hand.

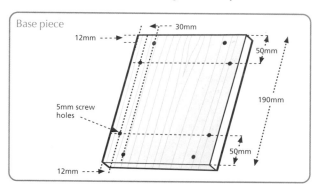

Base piece

30mm
12mm
50mm
190mm
5mm screw holes
50mm
12mm

6 Taking the piece of gravel board that will be the base, mark the location of the eight required 5mm screw holes. These need to be 12mm in from the edges, those at the sides being set back 50mm from the front and back faces, and those at the front and back set back 30mm from the sides. Drill and countersink these holes.

7 Drill and countersink two 5mm holes at both edges of the front and back pieces, 10mm in from the edge and 30mm in from each corner. Then fix one side piece in a workbench and, using two 2in x 8g screws, screw the back to it. Make sure the edges align as closely as possible.

TIP *Hold the back in place and mark 2mm pilot holes through the 5mm holes. Then remove the back and drill the 2mm holes deeper. These small pilot holes should prevent the wood splitting as the screws enter.*

8 Screw the rest of the box together using 2in x 8g screws for the sides and 1in x 8g screws for the base.

12 Align the front apex piece and mark the location of the holes for the dowel screws. Drill these holes with a 6mm bit. Fit the front apex into place.

If you're worried about the screw tips being sharp or protruding through the top of the apex saw them off – a metal cutting disc in a mini angle grinder is ideal for this job. See Chapter 1.

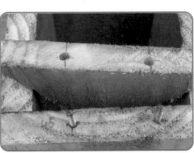

9 To make the removable roof, first mark and cut two 45° apex pieces as described in Steps 4 and 5 above.

Safety Cut these from long pieces of 150 x 25mm so that the wood can be held safely in the chop saw or else clamped securely when using a hand saw.

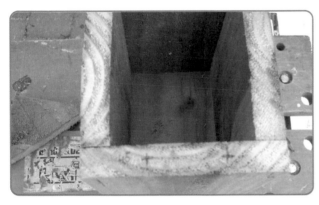

10 On the top edge of the box's front wall, mark two holes for the dowel screws that will locate the roof. Don't place these holes too near the sides or the dowel screws will protrude through the ends of the apex piece.

TIP *Increase the size of the 6mm hole a little by wobbling the drill bit around. This will allow the front apex to fit over the dowel screws more easily.*

13 Cut two 230mm lengths of 150mm feather-edge to form the roof.

11 Drill 4mm holes for each of the dowel screws and drive the screws in using a pair of pliers.

14 Rest the back apex in place against the back of the box and the front apex onto the dowel screws.

Rest one of the pieces of feather-edge on top of one side, with the thin edge at the top of the apex, and mark the fixing holes. The top screws are 20mm down from the top and the bottom ones are 80mm down from the top. Measure these marks carefully so that the screws are driven centrally into the edges of the two apex pieces and *not* into the apex section of the box's back wall.

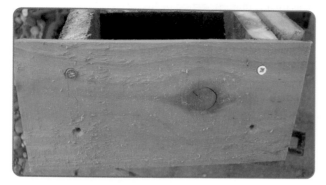

15 Drill and countersink 5mm fixing holes in both pieces of feather-edge and screw one length into place using 1in x 8g screws for the top and 1½in x 8g screws for the bottom (thicker) section. To ensure accuracy, carefully align the top of the first roof piece with the top of the apex pieces.

16 Fix the other side of the roof so that its top overlaps the first piece. The roof can now be lifted off.

17 Fit a small side latch to hold the roof in place.

18 Decide on the size of opening you want in the front of the box. This will depend on what type of bird you're trying to attract.

25mm holes for blue, coal and marsh tits, 28mm holes for great tits, tree sparrows and pied flycatchers, or 32mm holes for house sparrows, nuthatches and lesser spotted woodpeckers can be drilled using the appropriate size flat bit. 45mm holes for starlings can either be cut using a jigsaw (the birds won't care if they aren't round), a hole saw or an adjustable drill bit. For all of these, the hole needs to be about 150mm up from the base. These hole sizes apply for boxes with or without a removable roof, and they can be drilled after the box has been constructed.

Some species actually prefer an open-fronted nesting box. A 100mm tall front may attract robins or pied wagtails, a wren would need a front 140mm high, whilst spotted flycatchers prefer a front 60mm high. However, a box with a removable roof can't accommodate such a large opening.

Building a nesting box with a fixed roof

A nesting box with a fixed roof is much easier to construct. Other than cutting the front section with an apex exactly the same as the back section, follow Steps 1 to 8 above. Then cut the roof sections the same as in Step 13 and nail or screw the roof planks into place, using 30mm clout nails into the back and front apexes. Drill 2mm pilot holes in the roof sections to stop them spitting when the nails are banged in.

19 To cut the opening for an open-fronted box, mark the size you require and drill a 10mm hole in diagonally opposite corners for the jigsaw blade to fit into. Then cut carefully around the line to form the opening.

Safety Make sure the wood is securely clamped when cutting the hole.

Building a bat box

It is very important to select the timber treatment used for a bat box. Bats are highly sensitive to fumes given off by timber treatments, and the chances are that they won't survive if you use the wrong one. The box should be sited 4.5m to 6m above ground level and ideally not more than a quarter of a mile from a natural water source. An ideal location is sheltered, wind free, and exposed to the sun for at least part of the day. Under the eaves on a south facing wall is perfect.

1 Construct the bat box in the same way as the nesting boxes above, but don't cut a hole in the front.

2 Before the box is assembled you need to cut a slot in the base. First mark the location of the entrance – it needs to be about 20mm wide and located at the *back* of the box – and then drill a 16mm hole at each end of the marked slot.

3 Use a jigsaw to cut out the slot.

Building a nesting box with a curved roof

This nesting box with a curved roof has the disadvantage (or is it an advantage?) of the roof not being removable. This means that inspection of the nest isn't possible. However, the base can still be removed so that the box can be cleaned out when necessary.

Materials
- 1.3m of 150 x 25mm sawn timber for the main structure (gravel board could be used instead)
- Sufficient 12mm exterior grade plywood to make two 200 x 270mm roof pieces (do not cut them to size yet)
- 16 2in x 8g screws
- 40 1¼in x 8g screws
- Self-adhesive flashing
- Thin flexible batten to mark the roof curve
- 3 2in nails to hold batten
- Tree ties or wire to fix box

Tools
- Universal hard point saw
- Chop saw
- Circular saw
- Jigsaw
- Extension lead
- RCD (or safety plug)
- Belt sander/power sander
- Electric planer or hand plane
- Drill/driver
- Twist drill bits
  10mm
  5mm
  ⁵⁄₃₂in
  2mm
- Flat drill bits
  28mm
- Screwdriver bits
  Pozi (PZ) No 2
- Hammer
- Workbench
- Clamps
- Try square
- Combination square
- Pencil
- Tape measure
- Sharp knife
- Large (wallpapering) scissors
- Safety glasses
- Dust mask
- Ear defenders
- Gloves

Procedure

1 Cut two 200mm lengths of 150 x 25mm sawn timber to form the sides and two 320mm lengths to form the front and back. This should leave plenty of timber for the 100 x 150mm base. If necessary clamp the pieces together and plane the sides so that they are all the same width.

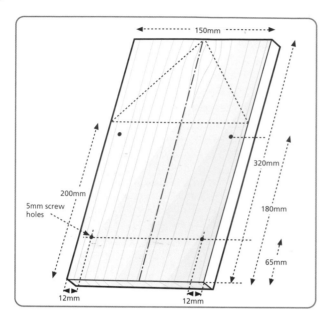

If the box is being fixed using wire, drill holes in the side pieces to thread the wire through (3mm holes should be large enough) at the same locations as the slots would be for straps.

Before the base is fitted, thread the straps or sufficient wire through the holes to wrap around the tree you've chosen.

2 Mark a line 200mm from one end of each 320mm piece. Then draw a centre line on both end pieces to cross the 200mm line, and draw a triangle from the centre mark to the 200mm marks.

3 Mark, drill and countersink four 5mm screw holes in the front and four more in the back. These need to be 12mm in from each edge and 65mm and 180mm up from the base. Take care that they don't coincide with the positions of the strap rebates described in the next step.

4 If the box is to be fixed in place with tree ties, mark the width of the tie on one 200mm edge of each side piece, 25mm and 150mm up from the bottom, ensuring that these positions don't coincide with the screw holes drilled in Step 3. Use a jigsaw to cut out rebates just deep enough (5mm) to fit the straps. Check that the strap fits into them.

5 You now need to cut the roof curve. Use a thin piece of batten as a guide to mark a slight curve on one edge of the front or back roof apex. Use three nails to hold the batten to the required curve and then draw the line. Don't make the curve too tight or the plywood roof won't bend sufficiently to fit it.

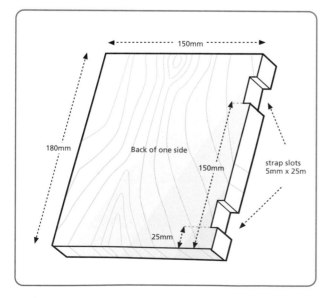

6 Cut along the curve using a jigsaw.

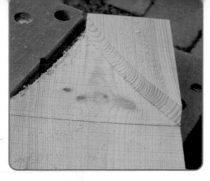

7 Use the offcut as a template for the curve on the other-edge and for the curves on the second apex.

8 Screw the sides and ends together using 2in x 8g screws. Before the screws are driven in drill a 2mm pilot hole into the edges of the sides through each of the 5mm holes. This will prevent the timber from splitting.

At this stage the entrance hole can also be drilled, but this isn't essential – it can be drilled later.

Making the roof

The roof is made from two 200 x 270mm pieces of 12mm exterior grade plywood cut from a larger sheet.

1 Mark the size of the roof onto the sheet of 12mm plywood – the sizes given allow for an overlap at the front

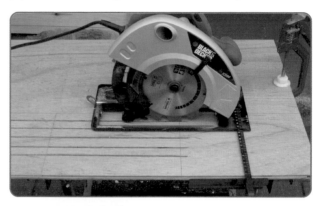

and the edges of the roof as well as taking into account the curve of the latter. Before cutting the two roof sections, cut grooves that will allow the plywood to bend. These shallow grooves are made 25mm apart on one side of the plywood, using a circular saw set to a depth of about 8mm so that it cuts all but one layer (ply) of the plywood (experiment on a spare piece first to ensure the cut isn't too deep). For safety, secure the plywood onto a flat surface before cutting the grooves.

TIP *Either secure one side piece in a workbench or else use some form of clamp to hold it in place while it's being fixed. Take care to align the bottoms of each of the four pieces before they're fixed.*

TIP *The circular saw's guide can be used to keep it the right distance from the edge.*

2 Drill and countersink a 5mm hole through each interstice between the grooves. It's important that these holes coincide with the centres of the front piece and back piece edges, which in this case would make them 12mm from the back and 210mm from the back.

Use 1¼in x 8g screws to fix the plywood to the curved apexes. Screw in each screw a little at a time to allow the plywood to assume its curvature gradually. The back of the roof should be flush with the box while the front should project to provide protection for the opening.

Making the base

The base provides the means of access to clean the box and therefore needs to be a push-fit. A few gaps round the edges won't be a problem – they'll provide drainage. The timber may be warped: if this is the case the base may need to be shaped to get it to fit.

1 Measure the size of the base opening (150 x 100mm) and cut a piece of 150 x 25mm timber to fit.

2 Drill and countersink two 5mm holes on either side (12mm up from the bottom and 50mm in from the edges) for the 2in x 8g screws that will secure the base.

Covering the roof

Self-adhesive flashing was used to cover the roof. When applying this, follow the manufacturer's instructions.

1 Before applying the roofing, plane or sand the ridge of the roof so that the join at the apex is smooth enough for the self-adhesive to fix to.

2 Cut four 330mm lengths of flashing, which should be long enough to wrap under the roof at the front. Cut one of these in half along its length.

3 Removing the protective paper as the flashing is pressed onto the plywood, stick the two half-strips into place on the underside of the roof eaves where they overlap the sides of the box. Then wrap them around each edge and onto the surface of the roof, taking care to fold the corners neatly. The next layers overlap these.

4 Apply another strip of flashing over each panel of the roof and then apply a final layer over the apex, overlapping the layers already applied. Take care to fold each layer under the overhang of the roof at the front and press it firmly into place against the body of the box.

Treatment

If you intend to treat the box use a non-toxic treatment (see Chapter 1 for more details).

Building a rabbit hutch

No hutch can be too large – the bigger the better! The hutch in this chapter is designed for two small rabbits. Two large rabbits would need a hutch of at least 1800 x 900mm total floor area and 900mm tall.

Any hutch needs two separate areas, and it should never have a wire floor – wire is not good for a rabbit's feet. It must also be secure against predators and escape. Bolts are better for this than turn buttons. The hutch needs to be located in a sheltered position and protected from prevailing winds.

Materials
- 19m of 50 x 25mm PSE
- 1220 x 2440mm sheet of 12mm WBP or exterior grade plywood
- 3.75m x 300mm self-adhesive flashing
- 600 x 900mm sheet of wire mesh for run doors
- 3m of 8.5 x 95mm TGV panelling for nest area doors
- Box of 100 1½in x 8g screws
- Box of 100 1¼in x 8g screws
- 12 4in x 8g screws
- 12 1in x 8g screws
- 6 2in x 8g screws
- 24 ¾in x 4g brass screws
- 16 galvanised wire staples
- 6m of shiplap cladding
- 3 barrel bolts
- 6 (3 pairs of) 1½in flush hinges
- Exterior grade filler
- Waterproof glue
- Extra durable varnish

Tools
- Universal hard point saw
- Tenon saw
- Chop saw
- Circular saw
- Jigsaw
- Extension lead
- RCD (or safety plug)
- Belt sander/power sander
- Electric planer or hand plane
- Drill/driver
- Twist drill bits
  5mm
  2mm
- Countersink bit
- Bradawl
- Screwdriver bits Posi (PZ) No 2
- Slot-head screwdriver
- Workbench
- Clamps
- Try square
- Combination square
- Pencil
- Tape measure
- Sharp knife
- Large (wallpapering) scissors
- Wire cutters
- Safety glasses
- Dust mask
- Ear defenders
- Gloves

Procedure

This hutch is 1400mm long x 600mm deep x 600mm tall.

Legs and framework

The legs are formed by fixing two lengths of 50 x 25mm PSE timber together to form an 'L' shape; sawn 50 x 25mm timber could also be used – it is less expensive and may look better in a garden – and in that case it could be treated, since the legs don't protrude inside the hutch and the rabbits wouldn't be able to chew them. However, the front inner support leg would need to be untreated.

3 Cut five 1070mm lengths of 50 x 25mm PSE and fix them together in the same way as in Steps 1 and 2 to produce the back legs. The fifth length is the back inner support leg.

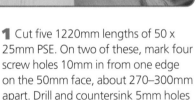

1 Cut five 1220mm lengths of 50 x 25mm PSE. On two of these, mark four screw holes 10mm in from one edge on the 50mm face, about 270–300mm apart. Drill and countersink 5mm holes at these marks.

2 Use 1½in x 8g screws to screw and glue each of these two drilled lengths to the 25mm face of two of the un-drilled lengths, taking care to align the ends and edges as they're screwed together. The resultant L-shaped pieces form the two front legs. The fifth 50 x 25mm length is the front inner support leg.

4 Cut a 560mm length of timber (50 x 25mm PSE is ideal) as a gauge for the height of the hutch floor. Use this to mark the height of the floor supports on the insides of the four legs and on the two support legs. Write 'bottom' on the appropriate end of each of the legs so that they're used the correct way up and the floor supports are fixed to the correct side of the line.

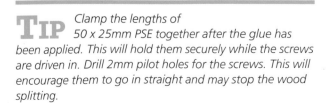

TIP *Clamp the lengths of 50 x 25mm PSE together after the glue has been applied. This will hold them securely while the screws are driven in. Drill 2mm pilot holes for the screws. This will encourage them to go in straight and may stop the wood splitting.*

5 Cut two 1400mm lengths of 50 x 25mm PSE. These run the full length of the hutch and act as front and back floor supports.

On a 50mm face at both ends of these, mark a line 25mm in as a guide to where to drill the screw holes. Using these marks as a guide, drill and countersink two 5mm holes at each end of each length. These floor supports will be screwed to the short (25mm) surface on the inside of the L-shaped legs.

6 Use 1½in x 8g screws to fix the front and back floor supports into place with their bottom edges against the 560mm floor-height mark made in Step 3. At this stage use only one screw at each end, to allow for adjustment.

7 Cut two lengths of 50 x 25mm PSE the full width of the hutch less the thickness of two pieces of 50 x 25mm PSE, therefore 600mm – (22 + 22mm) = 556mm. These form the end floor supports.

Hold one end floor support in place with one end resting against the side floor support on the 50mm face of the 'L'. Mark the position of the leg on the floor support as a guide to where to drill the screw holes.

8 Drill and countersink two 5mm holes in the 50mm face of both ends of each end floor support. Using one screw at each end, fix the end floor supports into place aligned with the front and back floor supports. The hutch is now taking shape but will be very wobbly.

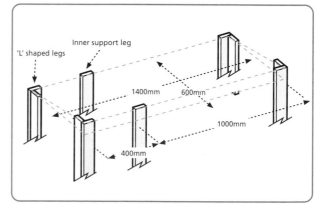

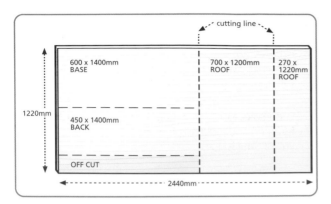

9 Mark and cut the sheet of plywood to form the floor, back, and roof. If possible get these cut by the merchant that supplies the plywood – they will then be very accurate. Write on each sheet what it's for.

10 Lay the plywood floor on the ground and stand the legs of the hutch so that they fit around its corners. Rest the back onto the floor supports. This will hold the frame square. The sheets of plywood are arranged this way to allow access to the fixing screws for the floor supports.

Use a try square to check the legs are at right angles to the end and front and back supports and drive in the remaining floor support screws.

11 When all four floor supports have been screwed into place, remove the plywood floor and back. Clamp the back and front inner support legs into place. Their centres

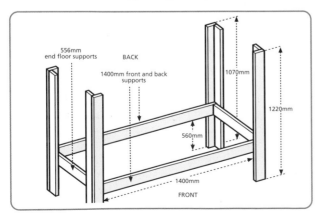

should be 400mm in from one end and 1000mm from the other. This position determines the size of the nesting area of the hutch and can be varied to suit you or the rabbits.

Use the 560mm gauge you made in Step 4 to check

that the inner support legs are at the correct height, and mark the position of the back and front floor supports on the inner support legs. Drill and countersink two 5mm holes and screw the support legs to the floor supports. Use a try square to ensure the inner support legs are square to the floor supports.

12 Drill and countersink a series of 5mm holes in each of the four sides of the 12mm plywood floor. These need to be 10mm in from the edge.

Apply glue to the top of the floor supports. Clamp the floor into place and drive in the 1½in x 8g screws.

13 Rest the plywood back into place and clamp the support legs so that they're upright. Using the legs and the inner supports as a guide, mark the plywood to indicate the location of the screw holes.

Remove the plywood and drill and countersink the 5mm screw holes (three holes for each leg and inner support). Screw and glue the back into place using 1¼in x 8g screws (longer ones will protrude on the other side of the legs).

Fitting the sides

The sides of this hutch are made using shiplap, but any other untreated cladding – including plywood – could be used. Treated timber should not be used since it could harm the rabbits if they chewed it.

1 Cut one piece of shiplap to length (for our hutch this was 590mm) and rest it in place at one end. If it doesn't fit adjust it until it does.

2 When it fits, cut another three lengths of shiplap for one end and four more for the other. Note that if they're all cut accurately to the same length they'll pull the legs square when they're screwed into place. Drill a 5mm hole in each plank close enough to the end so that a screw will go into the L-shaped legs.

TIP *The shiplap could be fixed (nailed or screwed) from the outside, but using screws on the inside hides the fixings and avoids the vibration caused by hammering in nails.*

3 Rest all the lengths of shiplap into place, make sure the grooves are pushed fully onto the tongues of the planks below, and screw the planks into place until the shiplap is level with the top of the back leg. Use 1¼in x 8g screws – longer ones will show on the outside. Likewise, take care to screw into the thick section of the shiplap so as to avoid the screws protruding through it.

Cutting the angle on the top of the legs

1 Clamp a straight edge to the tops of the legs to mark the angle of the roof. Use a try square to mark this line all round the top of each leg.

2 Saw the tops off to the marked line (a tenon saw may be easier to use for this job than a universal saw).

3 Rest a length of shiplap into place on top of the pieces already fitted at one end and use a straight edge to mark a cutting line on the shiplap to match the slope of the roof. Remove the shiplap and cut along the line. Repeat the process for the other end.

4 Cut a 50 x 25mm PSE top rail the same length (1400mm) as the front and back floor supports. This runs along the top of the hutch, at the front. Hold it in place and mark the locations for the screw holes at each end exactly as you did for the floor supports. Drill and countersink these 5mm holes. Using 1½in x 8g screws, screw the top rail into place on the narrow inside face at the top of the two front legs and the inner front support.

5 Mark the roof slope angle on both ends of the top rail, then remove the rail and use a straight edge to mark a line along one 50mm face. Plane the rail off to the marked line.

If you don't feel competent to do this, set the top rail lower down the legs so that the roof only touches it at the back edge.

6 Use a straight edge to mark the roof slope angle on the front and back inner supports and saw these off.

7 Hold the top (angled) section of shiplap in place at one end and mark the notch required to allow it to fit around the top rail. Then saw out the notch. Do the same for the other end.

Screw and glue the angled shiplap planks into place, clamping them until the glue dries. If you feel it

necessary, drive a small nail down through the top of the angle into the shiplap below.

Though it isn't good practice to glue boards together – they need to be able to expand and contract – in this instance it's acceptable.

Fitting the inner division

1 To support the partition between the nesting area and the run, screw a length of 50 x 25mm PSE inside the front inner support leg so that the plywood will sit flush with the run side. This length of PSE must be cut so that it doesn't protrude down into the opening between the nesting and run areas. Once fixed, it will also provide the stop onto which the nesting area door will close.

To support the back of the partition, a length of 50 x 25mm PSE is screwed vertically to the back of the hutch. This should screw into the back inner support.

2 Use offcuts of plywood to form the inner division. Make sure you don't use the plywood intended for the roof! For our hutch, two of these were 590 x 320mm and one was 420 x 270mm. Cut a notch in one of the 590mm pieces to fit around the top rail. Clamp this into place.

3 Mark the roof slope on the plywood using a straight edge as a guide. Cut the roof slope and screw the plywood into place, ensuring that its bottom edge is parallel with the floor so that the lower section will fit easily.

TIP *It helps if you screw the plywood into place before the angle is marked on it, so that it doesn't slip while it's being marked.*

4 Fix the second 590mm offcut into place under the first one to increase the depth of the division and form the top of the opening. This creates an opening 270mm high.

5 Decide on the width of the access between the run and nesting areas (for our hutch this was 180mm, but it may be dictated by the size of the available plywood offcuts) and fix a length of 25 x 50mm PSE to the plywood division already fixed into place to act as the middle support.

Mark and cut the 420 x 270mm offcut so that it fits below the second 590mm offcut and is the correct length to be fixed to the support. Screw it into place on the middle support.

The doors

All three doorframes are made using 50 x 25mm PSE glued and screwed at the corners. The two doors for the run have mesh fixed inside them and the door for the nesting area has TGV cladding fixed inside it. The doors are all the same height but may vary in width.

1 Measure the height of the door opening between the bottom of the top rail and the floor. For our hutch this was 560mm. Add 40mm to this to provide a 20mm overlap at the top and bottom of the door.

Cut six lengths of 50 x 25mm PSE the full height of the doors. For our hutch this was 600mm (see above).

Measure the total width of the run area (910mm) and halve it to find the width of the two run doors (455mm). Cut four pieces of 50 x 25mm PSE to form the tops and bottoms of the doors. Each piece will be half the width of the run, minus two widths of 50 x 25mm PSE (86mm).

Measure the width of the door for the nesting area. Cut two pieces of 50 x 25mm PSE to form the top and bottom of the nesting area door. These will be the width of the doorway (395mm) minus two widths of 50 x 25mm PSE (86mm) = 309mm long.

All the pieces having now been cut for the doors, it is a good idea to label them so that they don't get mixed up.

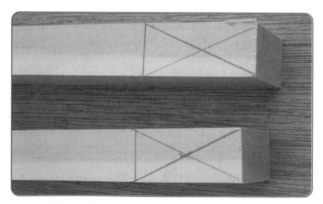

2 Lay out the pieces for one door on a suitable working surface and mark the ends of the six uprights carefully to indicate the width of the PSE. Draw diagonals to find the centre of these rectangles, then drill and countersink 5mm screw holes at these points.

3 The pieces for each doorframe are glued and screwed together. Use only one screw in each joint – there's a danger that two screws may split the wood. As usual, drill through each 5mm hole with a 2mm bit to make a pilot hole for the 4in x 8g screw. It may be necessary to remove one piece of wood from the clamp to drill the pilot hole a little deeper.

Check the diagonal to make sure the door is square – the diagonals should be identical. If necessary push the door into shape until the diagonals are the same. Then clamp it in place until the glue is dry.

4 When the glue is dry, hold the nesting area door in place so that it overlaps the front floor support and the top rail the same amount (about 20mm). Draw a line at top and bottom on the inside of the door to mark this overlap. This line will indicate where the panelling needs to stop.

While the door is still in place, mark on the back of it the location of the door stop formed by the 50 x 25mm PSE timber screwed to the partition.

Mark the location of the door on the top rail so that the doors for the run area can be aligned with the door for the nesting area.

Fixing the cladding to the nesting area door

The nesting area door is clad on the inside with TGV panelling, which will provide additional strength. This panelling will need to be cut to length and width.

1 Lay the door on a flat surface. Measure the length of TGV needed between the two lines marked in Step 4 of the previous section and cut the TGV to length.

2 Fit all the planks together (tongues into grooves) and mark the amount that needs to be removed from the edge planks so that together they're 20mm narrower than the door. This will allow the door to shut. Saw or plane the TGV planks to the correct width.

TIP *To get a neat job try to cut the same amount off both side planks – not all of it off just one plank.*

3 Remove a section of TGV from one edge of the cladding to allow it to fit around the doorstop marked earlier.

Screw and glue the planks into place, using one 1in x 8g screw in the top of each plank and two down each side. Do *not* glue the tongues and grooves together – apply glue only around the frame of the door. The grooved face needs to be facing outwards.

Lay the door flat and allow the glue to dry. Clamp it flat if necessary.

Fitting and adding the mesh to the run doors

Hold one of the run doors in place aligned with the marks on the top rail made for the alignment of the nesting area door. As with the nesting area door, mark along the top of the front floor support and the bottom of the top rail on the inside of the door to indicate where the mesh needs to stop. Mark the floor support rail and the top rail so that the other run door can be aligned. Hold the other door in place and mark it in the same way.

1 Lay the run doors flat and cut the mesh to fit. It needs to be just a little narrower than the doors and to fit between the top and bottom lines marked earlier. The mesh can be cut with wire cutters.

2 Cut four (two for each door) 15mm wide lengths of plywood as restraining strips for the top and bottom of the mesh. These will also add some strength to the corners of the door. Screw one of these strips into place using at least five 1¼in x 8g screws, two of which must go into the side pieces of the door.

3 Use galvanised staples to secure the sides of the mesh and screw the bottom restraining strip into place in the same way as the top one.

Check that the door fits into place. If it doesn't, adjust the top and bottom retaining strips until it does.

Fit the mesh to the other door in the same way.

Hanging the doors

The hinges must be fitted so that the ¾in x 4g brass screw heads fit into the countersink on the hinge.

1 The photograph shows the hinge used for alignment purposes. This is upside down so that the spine is resting on the edge of the door. To mark the location of the hinge, rest both hinges – the top of the top hinge 70mm down from the top of the door and the bottom of the bottom hinge 70mm up from the bottom of the door – on the door with the spine of the hinge touching the outside edge of the door. Use a pencil to mark the location of the holes in the inner (smaller) section of both hinges.

2 Use a 2mm bit to drill pilot holes for the ¾in x 4g screws. Screw the hinges into place on all three doors. Remove one hinge to use as a template.

3 With the hinges closed, hold a door in place aligned with the marks on the uprights. Make pencil marks on the uprights to mark the tops of both hinges, then open the template hinge and hold it aligned with one of the marks just made – but with the spine of the hinge about 1mm clear of the edge of the upright. Use a pencil to mark the location of the holes in both hinges.

TIP *If you drill the holes for the hinges in the wrong place, glue matchsticks into these holes. When the glue is dry, chisel them off and sand them.*

4 Fix all three doors, making sure that they line up along the top. It may be necessary to plane or sand a little off their edges to get them to fit. If so, before planing off any timber you should remove the retaining screw in the corner of the door and countersink it deeper, then replace it. This is so that the plane does not hit the screw head.

Fitting the hutch roof

It's easier to fit the roof after the doors have been hung. The bolts can be fitted at any stage.

1 Screw lengths of 50 x 25mm PSE to the inside of each end, to the partition, and to the back of the nesting area and the run. These are to fix the roof to.

The fixing battens on the shiplap are fixed using two 1¼in x 8g screws driven through holes in the batten into the shiplap. The fixing battens can be screwed to the plywood using 1¼in x 8g screws, driven through the plywood into the battens.

2 Cut a length of 50 x 25mm PSE to act as a support batten where the two sheets of plywood join. Use 1¼in x 8g screws through the plywood to fix this in place.

Rest the sheets of plywood in place on the top and clamp them there so that they're central. Remove any excess material from the small sheet if necessary.

Make sure that the plywood overlaps the hutch by the same amount at each end and at the back and front. For our hutch the end overlap was 55mm and the front and back overlap was 40mm.

3 Measure the location of the holes in the plywood carefully so that they coincide with the fixing battens and the tops of the uprights and the front piece. Then drill and countersink 5mm holes in the plywood so that it can be screwed to the uprights, each of the fixing battens, and the front piece.

Use 1½in x 8g screws to secure the roof to the fixing batten and the front piece, and 2in x 8g screws into the end grain of the uprights. Make sure all the screw heads sit below the surface of the plywood.

Applying the roofing material

The roof can be covered with felt (for details see the roofing section for the shed in Chapter 5), shiplap (see the roofing section for the kennel in this chapter), or one of any number of materials. The roof of our hutch is covered with 300mm wide self-adhesive flashing. It comes with a small tin of primer which can be used for porous or dusty surfaces but wasn't found to be necessary on the hutch.

1 Draw a line to indicate where the flashing will reach when it's tucked under the back of the roof. For our hutch this line was 263mm up the roof – 300mm less 25mm (the overlap at the back) and 12mm (the thickness of the plywood).

2 Use a damp cloth to wipe any dust from the plywood. Start applying the flashing at the back (bottom) of the roof. Cut the flashing so that it's long enough to fit under the ends of the roof. For our hutch this meant 1634mm long – 1500mm (the length of the roof) + 67mm at each end.

In order for the flashing to fit at the corners cut out a 30 x 67mm piece at each. Check this measurement carefully before cutting.

3 Stick the flashing in place, using the 263mm line made in Step 1 as a guide. Remove the protective backing paper as the flashing is applied to the roof. Smooth the flashing onto the roof and around the overlap at the bottom. Fold the corners into place.

> **TIP** *Remove the backing paper a little at a time, as the flashing is applied – do not pull it all off before the flashing is stuck down.*

4 Before you fit the middle piece of flashing, measure to establish where the front piece will reach to once it's tucked under the front edge of the roof. On our hutch this left a gap of 170mm between the bottom piece of

flashing, already applied, and the front piece. This would give an overlap of 65mm for each piece (300mm – 170mm = 130mm = 65mm + 65mm). Therefore mark a line on the bottom piece 65mm down from the top for the next layer to overlap to.

Cut the next layer of flashing to length and lay it to this line. Remove the backing paper and stick it into place. Smooth it around the overlap at both ends.

5 Draw a line on the second layer of roofing to mark the location (65mm down) of the final layer. Cut the final (topmost) piece of roofing to length and smooth it carefully into place.

Push all the corners into place until they're well stuck down and the roof is ready to repel the elements.

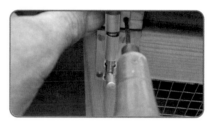

Door fastenings

1 Fix the three bolts to the doors using the screws provided. Either drill a small 2mm pilot hole for the screws or use a bradawl.

2 Take care that the bolt is located in the centre of the door stiles. Fit the bolt to the door first, then hold the receiver in place to establish its correct location before fitting it.

Finishing

1 Fill all screw holes with a good quality exterior filler, or plug them using a screw-sink and plug-cutter as shown in Chapter 1.

2 Sand off the filler and the woodwork. Protect the wood using stain or paint, taking care to ensure that it won't harm the rabbits if they should chew it. Our hutch used Sadolin Extra Durable Clear Coat , Clear – Satin. Do not treat the inside: it won't get wet so it doesn't need protection.

Garden Buildings Manual

DECKING

3

Most, but not all, decking structures are exempt from planning regulations. See Chapter 1 for more details. The Timber Decking Association (TDA) publishes a free leaflet (Ref TB 02) which gives the Planning and Building Regulations that apply to decks. In some cases the construction of steps to the decking is also governed by Building Regulations. Again, see Chapter 1 for further details.

Decide on the boundaries of your decking and mark them out. Drive in pegs if the ground is soft enough, make marks using chalk or a spray if not. Clear all vegetation and turf from the area and compact any soft ground, leaving a gentle slope *away* from any buildings to provide drainage. Lay a weed-suppressant membrane over any surfaces that may support vegetative growth. Cover this with a thin layer of gravel sufficient to hold it in place but not deep enough for weeds to grow in.

Establish the levels and decide if steps are needed and, if they are, where they're to be located.

Decide if the ends of the planks are to overlap the decking a little as in the project described below or whether a board is to be laid to hide the ends of the decking planks. Fitting a board will involve adding an additional joist to support the join between the ends of the joists and the edge of the board.

If you're working close to a house wall ensure that you don't bridge the damp-proof course.

Though there are many different ways of building a deck (the TDA website is a useful starting point), most consist of main support joists attached to vertical posts, with the decking planks fixed on top of the joists. The posts can be set into holes which are about 400mm deep and 300mm wide and filled with concrete, one post at each corner and the others at approximately 1500m intervals.

The joists are either fixed to the posts using bolts or are fixed into joist hangers which are fixed to additional support timbers. The joists must be set at the spacing recommended by the manufacturer of the decking planks: usually 400–600mm. The span (length) of the joists will depend on the size of the timbers. For a high level deck or complex decking a structural engineer should be consulted to advise on the correct design and timber sizes.

The decking boards are screwed to the joists using deck screws made from stainless steel, hot-dipped, galvanised or coated to British Standard specification BS7371 Part 6: the treatment used for the decking may react with the screws if they aren't suitably plated. The screws should be at least two times longer than the thickness of the decking board and positioned with two screws in each board into each joist.

The screws should be about 20mm in from the ends and edges of the decking boards and set into the groove in the board. To stop the board splitting and allow the screw to go into the timber easily, pre-drill the holes.

The decking boards need to be spaced about 5–10mm apart to allow for expansion when they get wet.

Materials

- 9 3.9m 100 x 50mm joists
- 11 4.9m and 10 4.2m 32 x 150mm grooved reversible deck boards
- 3 3.6m base rails
- 3 3.6m handrails
- 7 (R4A) 100 x 100mm newel posts
- 75 (R4A) 50 x 50mm spindles
- 4 3.6m lengths of 16.7 x 50mm fillet to fill in between the spindles at the base and handrails
- 1¼in round-head screws (8 for each bracket)
- ¾in galvanised nails or ¾in x 6g screws (one for each fillet in the base rail of the balustrade)
- 3in x 10g deck screws (quantity will depend on the decking design)
- 63mm deck screws (quantity will depend on the decking design)
- 5in x 12g plated screws (quantity will depend on the decking design)
- 100 x M8 bolts, washers and nuts (2 per newel post)
- 2 100 x M8 coach screws
- 150mm coach screws (FastenMaster) (quantity will depend on the decking design)
- 100mm coach screws (FastenMaster) (quantity will depend on the decking design)
- Brackets Large (Abru Joyner) (quantity will depend on the decking design)
- Wall plugs for fixing to base
- Timber preservative

Tools

- Universal hard point saw
- Chop saw
- Circular saw
- Jigsaw
- Extension lead
- RCD (or safety plug)
- Belt sander
- Electric planer
- Mains-powered electric drill
- Drill/driver
- Twist drill bits
  10mm
  6mm
  5mm
- Masonry drill bits
  10mm
  8mm
  4mm
- Flat drill bits – 16mm
- Screwdriver bits
  Square No 2
  Posi (PZ) No 2
  Posi (PZ) No 3
- Torque screwdriver bit
- Hammer
- Workbench
- Clamps
- Spirit level long
- Spirit level short (boat)
- Try square
- Combination square
- Pencil
- Tape measure
- Sliding bevel
- 13mm spanner
- Adjustable spanners
- 25mm (1in) chisel
- Mallet
- Safety glasses, dust mask, ear defenders & gloves

The decking described in this chapter was built in an 'L' shape around a conservatory. The base for the deck was a crazy paving patio that was uneven and in poor repair. Existing plants which were deemed important were tied back out of the way. The tumble-drier vent was no longer in use but was left there in case it was needed later.

Details regarding the regulations that must be followed and other structural considerations are given in Chapter 1.

Consider buying all the materials for this project from one supplier. This will help ensure compatibility of sizes. Our decking used material from Finnforest.

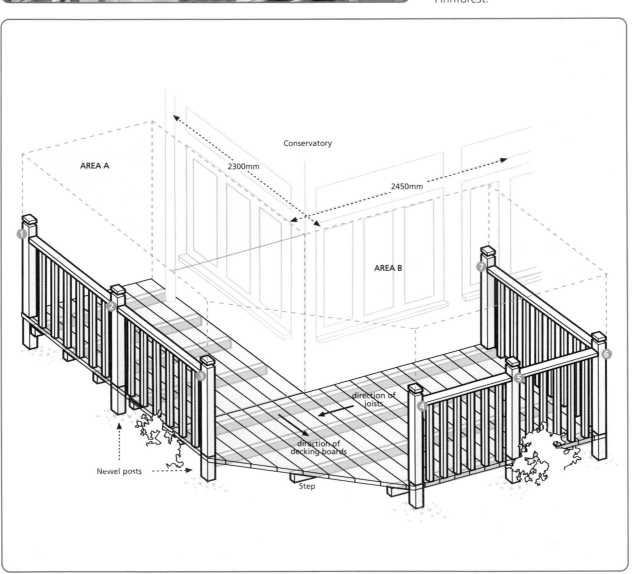

Planning

One end of the deck coincided with a back inlet gully (BIG) and a soil pipe, so the decking needed to be cut around the pipe and a maintenance hatch had to be fitted to allow access to the

BIG. The hatch consisted of two lengths of decking, cut to fit around the soil pipe and screwed to a fillet added to one side of the joist.

At the corner of the conservatory the deck was cut away to accommodate a wisteria, which was to be encouraged to grow to form shade for the south-facing conservatory. At the opposite end of the deck was a rambling rose which would be encouraged to ramble onto the decking balustrades, and an ornamental grass that would, eventually, grow up between the decking boards in that area.

One corner of the decking was cut at an angle to allow easy access around it and to form a step onto the patio.

The area was cleared – as much as the domestic requirements of the household would allow – and 100 x 50mm joist timbers were laid out to assess the slope and how uneven the paving was.

The 100 x 50mm joists were the laid out to establish a suitable spacing between them. For the decking boards used in this project the spacing was a maximum of 600mm between the centres of the joists. The approximate joist locations were marked on the paving with chalk.

TIP *Before planning the joist layout, check the required spacing of the joists with the decking supplier.*

A length of decking was used as a straight edge to establish the amount that the joists furthest from

the house needed to be raised – a slope of more than 25mm in 3m would be uncomfortable.

If the deck needed to be raised more than 200mm (8in), another step would have been needed in the corner. To avoid this, the joist nearest the house was cut down to a height of 60mm. This made a step of 230mm – 40mm, or 190mm (8½in), still too high for comfort, but the 25mm slope made the step 25mm lower, giving a total height of 165mm (6½in), a far more comfortable size.

The house wall was chosen as a datum line and the joists were aligned parallel to it. During this layout procedure it was established that the conservatory was not square with the house! This is important, since any irregularity in the shape of a building will influence the layout of adjacent

decking. Even a small discrepancy, if it had gone unnoticed, could have resulted in alignment problems along the front of the conservatory.

TIP *Use a 3 x 4 x 5 triangle to establish a right angle from the house wall.*

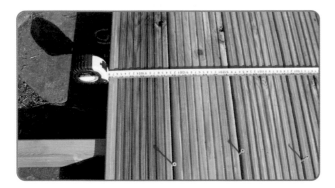

To establish the overall width of the deck, decking boards were laid out with the recommended 5mm spacing (this was achieved by placing a screw between the boards). The joists were cut in such a way that the decking boards would not need to be cut along their length to fit.

The width of deck along the front of the conservatory was calculated in the same way. On this deck the newel posts needed to avoid an opening window in the conservatory and a rose bush. This didn't allow much room for manoeuvre when deciding on the deck width. A rough measurement showed that 19 decking boards would be needed.

A skirting of decking boards was to be set around the deck between the newel posts to hide the joists. The decking boards would overlap this by 15mm.

TIP *A little extra width can be achieved by increasing the spacing between the decking boards by 1–2mm.*

Procedure

The following steps explain how the deck was constructed.

1 Stack the materials so that each item is easy to find. Space the timber to allow it to dry out – the balustrade spindles are ideal for this task. Stacking also makes it easier to check that the delivery is complete.

2 Cut the four 100 x 50mm treated timber joists for area A. These need to be long enough to support ten 141 x 25mm decking boards + 5mm spacing between each board and between the board edge and the wall = 146mm per board, or 1460mm for 10 boards. The length of the joist is therefore 1460mm less the overlap and the width of the skirting (1460mm – 15mm – 25mm = 1420mm). The decking boards will vary in size depending on the manufacturer.

3 The joists can be cut to length using a universal hard point saw, chop saw or circular saw. A few millimetres of timber can be removed using an electric planer. If they're being planed after they've been fixed, make sure the screw heads are a sufficient depth below the surface for the plane to miss them. When planing a joist make sure it's well secured before starting work.

To remove a lot of material, use a hand-held circular saw or a bench saw. See Chapter 1 for more details of how to cut the joists using a circular saw. In the case of the decking, there was so much material to remove along the length of the 50 x 100mm joists that it was cut off using a circular saw. When cutting timber using a circular saw always make sure the timber is well secured.

Cut the first joist – the one nearest the house – along its 100mm face so that it is 60mm deep, and lay it parallel to the datum wall. Lay the cut/planed face uppermost. The pressure treated section of timber should be on the bottom. The top face can be treated later.

4 To screw the joists to the paving, drill three 6mm clearance holes in the wood for the 5in x 12g screws. Hold the joist in place and use a long, small-diameter (4mm) masonry bit to drill down through the clearance holes into the paving. This will mark the location of the holes. Then remove the joists and drill the full-size holes (8mm for the wall plug being used) to the required depth.

An ordinary drill bit may not go all the way through 100mm deep timber. To overcome this, drill a clearance hole as deep as possible and then drive a screw into the hole until it comes out of the other side. This will mark where to start drilling a hole that will meet up with the original clearance hole. Better still, buy a drill bit long enough for the job!

TIP *If the screw is a little too short for the timber being fixed, drill a 16mm hole using a flat bit so that the screw can penetrate deeper into the wood. The screw should go into the wall plug to about three-quarters of the length of the plug.*

5 Check the newly fixed joist is level. If not, either remove some material from the top of the joist or pack it up a little. Use something that won't decay (*eg* lead, or a tile) and ensure the joist is packed (supported) at least every 600mm.

6 Use a straight edge, in this case a length of decking on edge, to check the level from the joist just fixed to the furthermost joist. Pack the furthermost joist up until it's level

TIP *Saw or plane each joist to size, rest it into place and check it's level. When it is, fix it to the paving.*

(or just a little lower, say 25mm, to allow for a fall) with the one just fixed. Pack the other end of this joist until it's level.

TIP *Timber used as a straight edge should be used on edge, not flat – there's less chance of it bending when on edge.*

7 Use the straight edge to measure the depth required for the remaining joists. Check that the straight edge is level and measure down to the paving at the location of the next joist. This will give the depth of the joist at that point.

Do the same at the other end, making sure the straight edge is still level after it has been moved.

Alternatively, instead of measuring the distance between the bottom of the straight edge and the paving, stand a piece of timber on the paving so that it is resting against the straight edge, and mark the timber where it touches the bottom of the straight edge. This will give the distance between the bottom of the straight edge and the paving.

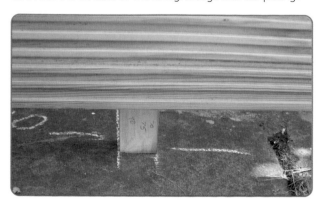

8 Use a 3 x 4 x 5 triangle to check that the ends of the joists are at right angles to the wall. To do this, mark off 3ft along the wall and 4ft on a length of decking board. Measure the distance (hypotenuse) from the 3ft and 4ft marks and adjust the decking board until this distance is exactly 5ft – the board will then be at right angles to the wall. Align the ends of the joists with the decking board.

9 Lay the four long joists in place in area B, taking care to align both ends. Check the overall length of the joists to establish how many decking boards are needed. Ten boards (area A) + 14 boards = 24 boards = 146 x 24 = 3504mm (the 5mm difference for one missing gap won't matter over this distance). Cut the joists to this length, allowing for the overlap and the skirting.

10 Use a straight edge to check the level from joist to joist. Prop up the ends of the joists until they're level from end to end and from joist to joist. When this has been done check that the ends of the joists are still aligned.

If it isn't, remove any excess timber until it is. Small amounts can be planed off. Treat the exposed timber. If it's necessary to build the front of the step up cut another length of timber to support it.

13 Mark the angles on the 100 x 50mm step front and cut them. Treat the ends before fitting it. In this case, as the step front would be hidden by the skirting a coloured timber treatment was used.

11 Lay a straight edge across the corner of the decking that will form the step to establish what angle looks best. When the angle looks right, mark it onto both the joists. Cut these angles using a chop saw or a universal hard point hand saw.

12 Realign the joists that have been cut for the step and lay a section of 100 x 50mm joist against the angles to represent the front of the step. Check that this is level.

14 Align the joists and the step front, making sure all the ends line up and the spacing is correct.

16 Screw the front of the step into place with 4in x 10g plated screws, taking care to keep the joist aligned correctly.

TIP *Drill 5mm holes into the step so that the screw goes straight into the end grain of the joist, not at an angle to it.*

15 One end of the decking joists spanned a border and rested onto a flagstone. The flagstone was too good to drill holes in, so a concrete pad was cast next to it. To do this, dig a shallow (200mm deep) trench and fill it with concrete (ratio 4:1 – see Chapter 1 for more details about concrete). The height of the concrete pad can be increased by using bricks or old paving slabs. In this case two sections of edging stone were rested on top of the concrete (one was later removed). Insert a strip of wood to prevent the flagstone getting covered in concrete.

17 Lay the joists in place and plug and screw three of them (not the one behind the wisteria) to the paving, using 150mm coach screws or similar. Counter-bore the drill holes using a 16mm flat bit to set the head of the screws below the surface of the joist. This will also allow the screw to go deeper into the plug in the paving.

The joist behind the wisteria was propped so that it was level with the first joist and level along its length.

18 Rest a straight edge on the first joist (by the house) and the outermost joist. Clamp a short length of timber (serving as a level gauge) to one end of the straight edge so that it rests on top of the outermost joist. Adjust this until the straight edge is level.

19 Measure the amount of the level gauge that's protruding from under the straight edge. Note this measurement and undertake the same exercise on the other end of the outermost joist and the wisteria joist. Remove 25mm from the measurement to allow for the slope of the decking. These two measurements represent the depth

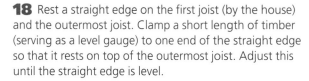

of the packing piece (firring piece) required to rest on top of the outermost joist to level it.

Mark a 4.2m length of 100 x 50mm treated timber using the measurements established using the level gauges. Draw a straight line between these marks along the length of the timber and cut to this line using a circular saw or a planer.

TIP *The firring piece can be made in two or three sections – it doesn't have to be in one piece. However, if it is of more than one piece you should number them so that they can be located on the correct joists.*

20 Rest the cut length of the firring piece onto the joist and check for levels. If the levels are correct, screw it into place.

21 Cut and fix the other firring pieces to level the other joists, except for the one behind the wisteria.

22 Mark the angle for the step onto the firring piece on the outermost joist. Cut this angle using a chop saw or a universal hard point saw and replace the firring piece. Do the same with the firring piece at the other side of the step.

23 Cut and trim a firring piece to fit on top of the step, level with the joist firring pieces, to raise the level. Screw it into place.

24 Make a final check of levels and remove any excess timber. Check that the screw heads are set far enough into the timber not to be cut by the planer.

25 The paving under the joist along the conservatory wall by the wisteria was so uneven that the joist was screwed directly to the flagstones in some places, while in others it was fixed using Abru Joyner brackets screwed to the paving.

26 Lay a weed suppressant membrane over any areas of soil that may support the growth of plants. Cover this with a shallow layer of gravel to keep it in place.

27 Treat all the cut areas of timber with a suitable preservative.

Fixing the newel posts and balustrade

It isn't essential to fit a balustrade unless the decking is high enough to pose a danger if someone should fall off it – in which case Building Regulations come into force and adequate protection will be required.

Decking tends to be used as a communal area, and if people gather on the deck some will lean against the balustrade or even sit on it. For this reason it needs to be firmly secured.

The newel posts on our decking were fixed in two different ways, depending on the direction of the joists. None of them was fixed to the house or the conservatory.

Newel posts numbers 1, 2, and 3 in area A were fixed to the side of the joist. They overlapped the end of the joist enough to allow for the skirting and a 15mm overlap. Post 1 was fixed to a 60mm-high joist which offered little support. To overcome this a bracket was used.

Newel posts 2 and 3 were fixed to the joists using two coach screws (in this case 4in FastenMaster type) per joist.

Newel posts 4, 5 and 6 were fixed to the side of the front (outermost) joist. These needed a section (rebate) cut out to allow them to fit over the joists. The corner newel (post 6) overlapped at both faces of the deck, front and end.

Newel post 7 was fixed to the joist using two 150mm x 12g screws.

TIP *The newels could be set into post spurs (see the gazebo section of Chapter 4). This would give them more support than simply fixing them to a narrow joist.*

---

1 Before the newel posts are fixed you need to decide on the height of the handrail above the deck (for our decking it was 900mm).

To assess the length of the newel post, undertake a dummy run. Lay a newel post flat and rest the following on it: a length of decking; a short length of 100 x 50mm (used as a spacer to lift the base rail off the deck); a short length of base rail; a spindle; and a short length of hand rail. This will indicate the overall height of the handrail above the decking. Decide on the length of newel post that will protrude above the handrail – for our decking this was 150mm.

Cut the spindles to a suitable length.

Measure the total length from the top of the newel post to the bottom of the decking board.

If the decking is high above ground level, the height of the balustrade will be dictated by Building Regulations.

2 Cut the newel posts to length. This will be the length from the top of the newel post to the underside of the decking board plus the height of the joist at the post's intended location.

TIP *Use a combination square to find the depth of the joists.*

3 Clamp the cut-to-length newel posts into place and rest a straight edge across their tops to verify that they're level.

4 For newel posts with a rebate (numbers 4, 5 and 6), cut the post to length and stand it in place alongside the joist. Mark the top of the joist onto the newel. Measure the depth of the rebate carefully. The thickness of timber left on the newel is the thickness of the skirting (25mm) + the overhang of the decking boards over the skirting (15mm) = 40mm.

TIP *Clearly identify with a pencil squiggle the wood that's to be removed – it's very easy to cut out the wrong piece of timber!*

5 Make a mark 40mm in from one side of the newel post. Use a try square to ensure that your marks are square around the newel. Make the top cut first – the section that rests onto the joist.

6 Cut the other (long) cut to meet the top cut. Remove the posts and stand their cut ends in timber treatment for ten minutes or so.

TIP *Take care to keep the cut along the line. Cut from one side then turn the post over and cut from the other side – this should help to keep the cut aligned. Treat the cut area before fixing the post.*

7 Fix the rebated newel posts to the sides of the joists using 100 x 8mm (M8) bolts with washers and nuts.
  Newel post 4 was fixed with one 100 x M8 bolt and a 100 x M8 coach screw, since there was no space for a nut on the sloping section of the step.

9 Check the newel posts are upright as they're erected – if they're not the balustrade will be very difficult to fit. To ensure a newel post is vertical in one plane (direction), use just one fixing initially, so that the post can be pushed upright;

then clamp or prop the post into place and drill the second fixing hole. Check that the newel is still upright, then tighten the fixings.

In the other direction, it's the twisting of the joists that allows newel posts to move off the vertical. Once the decking boards are secured to the joists they'll hold the newel more rigidly.

8 For newel posts 2 and 3, conventional coach screws were too large to use so close to the ends of the small sections of timber. FastenMaster coach screw equivalents were used instead, since being much smaller

in diameter they were less likely to split the timber. Pre-drill the holes to ensure that the screws are in the correct place.

TIP *Prop the newels upright as the decking is screwed into place. The decking boards add a lot of support to joists that the newels are fixed to.*

10 If the newel posts aren't upright and can't be fixed to stay that way, cut wedges and use these to hold them erect. The wedges can be cut off flush with the joist and left in place, so that the decking boards will fit over the top if necessary.

Skirting

Skirting, made using decking boards, is added around the sides of the deck to hide the joists. Trim it to follow any fluctuations in the ground so that it's level when fitted. In some places more than one piece of skirting may be needed to fill the gap between the decking and the ground. When this happens fit the top piece first, so that it is level with the joists, and then cut the lower piece to fit between it and the ground.

TIP *If the fixing bolts stick out from a newel and interfere with the block, hold the block in place and hit it with a hammer so that an imprint of the fixings is made on it. Then drill shallow 10mm holes at these indentation marks to allow the block to sit flush.*

1 Set the skirting boards in from the face of the newel posts by about 15mm to allow the decking boards to overlap. Note that it's best if the skirting doesn't actually touch the ground – if it does it will soak up the damp.

2 Where the skirting covers the ends of joists, screw it to them using deck screws. Where there is no joist, screw an offcut block to the side of a newel post using 63mm deck screws and fix the skirting to this. Use the holes drilled for the newel fixing bolts as a guide to where *not* to drill the 6mm fixing holes for the block. Check that these blocks don't protrude above the top of the joists.

3 All cut faces of these timber blocks should be treated. A clear solution was used on the decking to allow it to remain its original green.

4 Cut each section of skirting to length. Do *not* make them a tight fit – it's necessary to allow for expansion as the timber gets wet.

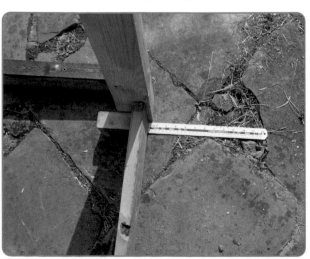

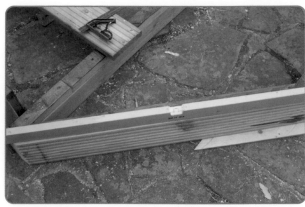

Hold the length of skirting in place and check that it doesn't push the newel post off the vertical.

The grooves in the skirting must be horizontal. To ensure this, prop the skirting board level and mark it to fit the contours of the ground. Cut to this line and screw it into place using 63mm deck screws.

TIP *If using reversible decking take care to get it the correct way round. Treat the cut areas of skirting.*

5 At the step, you must cut the skirting at an angle to fit. Hold it in place and mark the required angle. Once cut, rest this piece into place and check that it fits.

6 Cut the skirting to the required angle, then try it in place. Check that it's level. If it isn't, scribe it to fit.

7 Clamp the skirting into place and check that the grooves in the board are horizontal. Drill 6mm holes and screw it to the step joist using 63mm deck screws.

8 Once the skirting has been fixed plane off any excess.

9 Fit the uppermost section of skirting first. Cut the lower section of skirting to fit, using a jigsaw or a planer. Treat all cut ends and edges and, using 63mm deck screws into pre-drilled holes, screw the skirting into place, ensuring

that it's level and flush with the top of the joists. Cut wedges to prop the skirting off the ground while it's being screwed into place.

Safety If cutting it with a circular saw ensure that the skirting is held firmly in place while it's being worked on.

Fitting the decking

Once the newel posts have been fitted (if required) and the skirting has been fixed, the decking boards can be laid.

1 Lay the first length of decking in place, resting against the newel posts. Use a try square to mark where the board needs to be cut to fit around the posts. Don't make this a tight fit – allow 2mm either side of the post.

2 Use a combination square to mark the depth of the cut needed, and allow 2mm extra. Mark this on the decking board.

3 Use a universal/hard point saw to cut along the two lines that form the side of the cut-out. Take care not to cut beyond the line that marks the back of the cut-out.

4 Ensuring that the board is securely clamped, use a flat bit to drill a 16mm hole near one corner of the cut-out.

5 Use a jigsaw to cut from that hole to the back line.

6 Turn the saw around to cut along the back line.

7 Push the board into place round the newel posts and check that it's still square with the datum house wall using a 3 x 4 x 5 triangle.

TIP *The short length of timber on one side of some cut-outs will break off easily. Take care not to force it around the newel post.*

It's better if the ends of the boards don't touch the wall of the house. Cut a length of timber to act as a gauge to space all the decking boards the same distance from the wall.

8 Screw a length of timber alongside the second joist out from the house wall, to act as a support for the two short, removable, lengths of decking that fit around the soil pipe.

9 Lay out the rest of the boards to cover that area. If using reversible decking boards make sure they're all the same way up.

10 Screw the boards into place. The screws need to be 20–25mm in from the edge of the board and fitted into the groove. Use two screws through the board into each joist. The boards need to be spaced at least 5mm apart (check the suppliers' requirements) – drive a deck screw into a length of wood so that it can be used as a spacer.

The decking will add rigidity to the joists that support the newel posts. If the posts aren't vertical, prop or wedge them so that they are before the decking is fixed. This will help to hold them in place

11 In area A, fix the length of decking that's closest to and parallel with the wall of the conservatory. This can be done because the spacing for the boards was carefully calculated when the joists were cut to length.

Cut the two boards closest to the conservatory wall so that they rest on the joist near the soil pipe and not the support timber fitted earlier. This will allow room for the short lengths of decking that fit around the pipe.

The other boards between can be spaced to fit. If the boards are bowed, they may need to be forced to achieve the correct spacing. Use a wedge to force boards towards or away from each other.

TIP *To drill your screw holes in the right places, use a length of decking board as a straight edge to mark where the joists are.*

12 Use a combination square to mark the area that needs to be removed from the decking board that fits around the newel post at the other side of the step.

13 The rest of the decking can be laid and fixed into place until the far end is reached. Cut around each newel post and any obstacles (such as the wisteria) as the work proceeds.

14 Trim and fit the final length of decking around newels 6 and 7. Check all the deck screws have been driven in fully.

TIP *The ends of the decking boards don't need to be trimmed at this stage – it's easier to trim them to length later.*

15 Make a cardboard template to mark the hole that needs to be cut to fit it around the soil pipe.

16 Use a jigsaw to cut the hole in the two short pieces of decking that fit round the pipe.

17 Fit and screw these pieces into place around the soil pipe and to the support joist.

18 Use a straight edge as a guide to mark where the edge of the decking needs to be trimmed. This can be rested against the outside of the newel posts.

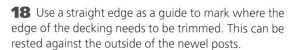

TIP *Use a ruler (such as the blade of a combination square) pushed between the decking boards to locate the edge of the skirting and measure the 15mm overlap from this.*

19 The excess decking can be cut off using either a universal/hard point saw…

20 …Or a circular saw run along a fixed straight edge (measure from the edge of the saw plate to the blade carefully in order to set the straight edge in the correct place)…

21 …Or a jigsaw run carefully along a marked line.

22 Use a belt sander to sand off the rough edges.

Balustrade rails and spindles

The balustrade consists of a handrail with a rebate cut into the underside for the spindles, and a base rail with a rebate in its upper surface. It is recommended that the base rail is set above the decking to allow easy cleaning.

This section also deals with fitting a balustrade between the posts of the pergola constructed in Chapter 4.

The base and hand rails are fixed as follows:

- to newel post 1: brackets (there's no access from the back of the post).
- to newel post 2: screws through the post on one side and brackets on the other, less obvious, side.
- to newel posts 3 and 4: screws through the post. These are the posts on either side of the step, with rails on only one side. Plug the holes left by the screws.
- to newel post 5: screws through the post on one side and brackets on the other, less obvious, side.
- to newel post 6 (a corner newel): screws through the post on both sides. Plug the holes left by the screws.
- to newel post 7: brackets (there's no access from the back of the post).

TIP *Plan the order of fixing the rails carefully so that they aren't put in place too soon, preventing holes being drilled for the fixing on the other side of the newel post. A similar plan needs to be made for fitting the rails between pergola posts.*

1 It's essential that the newel (or pergola) posts are upright at this stage – if they are the base rail and the handrail will be the same length. If the posts aren't upright it will be difficult to get the spindles to look vertical when they're fitted. It may be necessary to wedge or prop the posts to keep them upright.

2 Measure the length required for each base rail carefully, cut it to fit, and rest it onto a short length of joist material laid flat to raise it off

the deck. Use a short spirit level (boat level) to check that the base rails on two sides of the posts are level.

3 Use a boat level or try square to check that the base rail is level across its width. Check the base rail is level from one post to the next. All irregularities should be rectified.

4 Mark the rebate in the base rail on the post. Use this mark to locate the screw holes and drill 6mm holes for the 5in x 10g screws that will hold the rail in place.

TIP *It's not easy to drill holes at right angles unless a guide is used. To overcome this problem, drill from the side that the rail's to be fixed to – if the holes are at an angle they'll be in the right place to go into the rail.*

5 Rest the base rail in place on the spacing blocks and ensure it's aligned with the marks.

6 If one end of the base rail is to be fixed using a bracket, screw the bracket into the rebate of the base rail using 1¼in x 8g round head screws before the rail is fixed. Hold the rail firmly, check it's level, and screw it into place. If countersunk screws are to be used the holes in the bracket will need to be countersunk so that the heads fit flush to the surface.

If the grey colour of the brackets is a little too obvious they can be covered with a metal paint.

7 As the base rails are fitted use a try square to check that they're aligned with each other on either side of the posts.

8 Cut a 50mm length of spindle to fit between the decking and the centre of the base rail as a support.

9 Cut the handrail to length. If the posts are upright this will be the same length as the base rail. If the handrails are too long they'll push the posts off vertical. Check that this hasn't happened as each handrail is fitted.

10 Cut the spindles to the length decided on at the planning stage (see page 82). Rest three or four cut spindles in the rebate of the base rail and against the two newel (pergola) posts. Rest the handrail in place on top of these spindles and mark the location of the underside of the handrail on the newel (pergola) posts.

11 Clamp a length of timber level with the marks made for the underside of the handrail.

12 Rest the handrail on this and mark its location.

13 Screw the brackets into place and fix the handrail in the same way as the base rail.

14 Estimate how many spindles are needed between each two posts. Building Regulations for stairways come into play here: Part K states that the spindles should be no more than 100mm apart.

> **TIP** The spindles can be inserted after the base rail and handrail have been fitted if they're put in at an angle. To space the spindles, place them onto the base rail at approximately 100mm intervals and see how many are needed. Adjust the spaces until they're all the same. 100mm lengths of spindle offcut can be used as spacing guides.

15 Measure the distance between the spindles carefully and cut the number of fillets required for both the base and hand rails to this exact length. Bear in mind when cutting them that just 1mm added to each fillet will give an inaccuracy of as much as 12mm over twelve spaces – which is quite a lot. It's also important that the top fillets are the same length as the bottom ones – if they're not then the spindles won't be vertical.

> **TIP** Cut half the number of fillets required for the base rail, put them in place and check they take up half the width between the newel posts. If they do cut the other half, if they don't adjust the size. Cut all the fillets to the same length.

16 The bottom fillets can rest in place in the rebate of the base rail. However, the top fillets need to be nailed or screwed into place. Use ¾in galvanised nails or ¾in x 6g screws for this. Drive one into the fillet first, then hold the fillet in place and drive the nail or screw into the handrail. Don't drive the nails in fully to start with, just in case they're not quite the right length. Once all the fillets have been fitted and the spindles are vertical then they can be driven in fully.

Finishing touches

Glue wooden plugs into all the exposed screw holes – see Chapter 1 for more details. When the glue is dry chisel the plugs off to length or cut them off using a tenon saw. Use a belt sander to sand the plugs until they're flush with the surrounding surface.

Stain the deck to the required colour. Our deck was left for a few months to fade and then treated with a clear stain.

GAZEBO AND PERGOLA

4

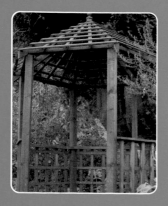

Building a gazebo

The gazebo in this chapter was built 1.9m diameter and 2.24m high so that it would fit into an area between trees and shrubs, but within reason a gazebo can be built to any size you like.

Lay out the floorplan of the gazebo in the area in which it's to be built. Check that the area is level and remove any debris.

Initial stages

1 Drive a stake into the ground at the centre of the gazebo base.

2 Using a piece of string the radius of the gazebo (in this case 950mm), mark out a circle denoting the ground area it will occupy.

Safety Check that there are no gas pipes, power cables or water pipes running through this area.

Materials
- 6 3m lengths of 75 x 38mm treated timber
- 6 2.4m 75 x 75mm fence posts
- 6 post spurs (if required)
- About one small bag of gravel per post (only needed if spurs are not used)
- One small bag of cement (only needed if spurs are not used), or one small bag of cement/gravel mix per spur, or one small bag of Postmix (rapid set) per spur
- 12 4in x 10g screws
- 24 3in x 10g screws
- 24 2½in x 8g screws
- Box of 100 1½in x 8g screws
- Box of 100 1in x 6g screws
- 8 1½in x 5mm coach screws
- 500gm of 50mm oval galvanised nails
- Timber treatment
- Finial for the roof (a Metpost finial was used for our pergola)
- 50 63mm deck screws
- 6 5in x 12g screws
- 8 plugs for bolt-down spurs
- 8 washers and bolts for bolt-down spurs
- 5in x 12g yellow zinc screws
- 3in x 10g deck screws

Tools
- Universal hard point saw
- Tenon saw
- Chop saw
- Circular saw
- Extension lead
- RCD (or safety plug)
- Belt sander
- Electric planer or hand plane
- Mains-powered electric drill with hammer action
- Drill/driver
- Twist drill bits 6mm 5mm 4mm
- 10mm masonry bit
- Screwdriver bits Posi (PZ) No 2 Square No 2
- Hammer
- Claw hammer
- Large hammer, sledge or lump
- Spur dolly
- Workbench
- Clamps (at least 2)
- Spirit level long
- Spirit level short (boat)
- Try square
- Combination square
- Set square
- Pencil
- Pair of compasses
- Tape measure
- Sliding bevel
- 13mm or adjustable spanner
- 2 pairs of step ladders or tower scaffold
- Safety glasses
- Dust mask
- Ear defenders
- Gloves

Making the roof

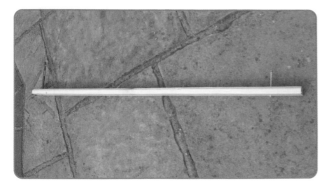

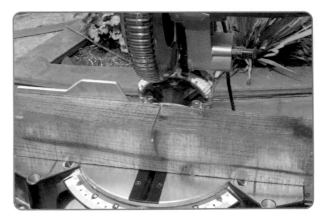

1 Mark out a flat area on which the roof can be built, the same size as the gazebo base – for instance the garage floor, a patio or an area of lawn – a piece of wood with a screw in one end and a pencil through a hole in the other can be used for this. Place the screw on the circumference of the circle and make a mark on the circumference with the pencil. Work around the circle, moving the screw to the mark previously made, until you've made six marks. These will be the six points of the gazebo's hexagonal roof.

2 Use a straight edge and a pencil to draw straight lines between these marks.

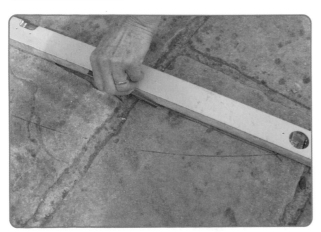

3 Cut six 300mm lengths of 75 x 75mm fence post.

4 Stand these short lengths at the points of the hexagon. These act as short posts on which to build the gazebo roof.

5 Measure the distance between each post and adjust the posts until they're all the same distance apart but still as close as possible to the circumference marks (950mm).

6 Cut six 75 x 38mm wall plates to fit on top of the posts – for our gazebo these were 950mm long, but check this length carefully. Cut a 30° angle at both ends of each.

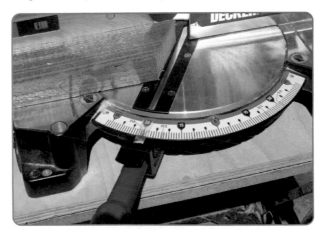

This is the correct angle to form a hexagon, and the wall plates will fit snugly together if the angles are cut accurately. Check carefully to make sure the first three fit together on top of the posts. When they do, cut the other three using the first ones as a template.

8 Level the posts all around and check the diagonals are all the same. Push the hexagon into shape if necessary and screw the wall plates to the tops of the posts. Re-mark the location of the posts.

7 Draw a diagonal on the top of each post and align the wall plates with it. It's important that this alignment is accurate, otherwise fitting the trellis and handrails will be difficult.

9 Drill 5mm holes in both ends of each wall plate for the 3in x 10g deck screws and screw them to the posts. To ensure accuracy, mark the locations of the screw holes before drilling them, to ensure that the screws will be going into a part of the posts where there's plenty of timber to accommodate them.

TIP *To avoid drilling into the tops of the posts themselves, rest a piece of plywood or an offcut under the area to be drilled.*

Making the hexagonal centre support

The rafters join onto a hexagonal centre post at the centre of the roof.

1 Use a pair of compasses to draw a circle with a 37mm radius (a diameter of 75mm) on a stiff piece of paper. Then, with the compasses still set at 37mm, make six marks around the circumference.
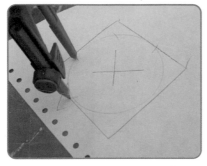
Join these marks to form a hexagon and cut it out.

2 Cut a 150mm length of 75 x 75mm timber from the top of one of the 75 x 75mm uprights and sand the sides and ends smooth enough to make it easy to draw a pencil line on them.

3 Stick the paper hexagon on one end of it, if possible with one face of the hexagon resting along one of the sides of the timber and the hexagon corners touching the edges of the timber where possible.

Safety When sanding or planing the 75 x 75mm timber be sure it's securely held, *eg* in a workbench.

4 Where the corners of the hexagon touch the edges of the timber, draw lines along the length of the timber to act as a guide to the position of the hexagon at the other end. If the ends are cut square, a try square can be used as a guide for these lines. Alternatively, use a combination square to mark the distance from the edge of the timber. Draw the hexagon at the other end.

5 Plane the corners off to these lines using a power plane or hand plane. It may be necessary to redraw some of the lines as the planing progresses. Each of these planed faces forms one side of the hexagon. Sand the final 2mm or so to ensure accuracy and a flat surface.

Finding the correct angle for the apex of the rafters

1 Cut one 3m length of 75 x 38mm timber in half to form rafters and lay the two 1.5m lengths on a flat surface, one end resting on top of the other. Adjust the angle until you find the one that suits you. The steeper the angle of the roof the higher the gazebo will be, so if there's a height restriction you'll need to bear this in mind. The angle chosen for our gazebo was 32°.

2 Set the sliding bevel and mark this angle on the ends of the rafters. Mark the sliding bevel setting onto a piece of wood and label it, so that it can be reproduced if the setting should get accidentally moved.

3 Using a universal/hard point saw or a chop saw, cut this angle on one end of both rafters. The angle will be altered later once the foot of the rafter has been cut.

4 Clamp the pair of rafters together so that the feet are resting on the corners where two wall plates join and the two angles are touching at the top (apex). This arrangement can be set on a post clamped into a workbench.

The foot of each rafter can be cut so that it either rests on the wall plate or fits over it. The latter is called a birdsmouth. A rafter without a birdsmouth is more straightforward but, to my mind, doesn't look as pleasing as a rafter with one. Our gazebo is therefore built with birdsmouthed rafters.

Without birdsmouth

With birdsmouth

Cutting rafters without a birdsmouth

1 Mark lines on each face of the hexagonal centre post, 30mm from one end. These lines can then be used to align the tops of the rafters. The 30mm distance is to allow for trellis or roofing.

2 Drill a 5mm hole into the top of one rafter so that the screw will go into the hexagonal centre post at right angles to the post. Hold the centre post in place and screw the first rafter to it so that the top of the rafter is 30mm down from the top of the post.

3 Screw another rafter into place on the centre post. This will support the post while the angles on the feet of the rafters are being marked. Mark the rafters so that they can be relocated easily, *eg* letter them A and B with a pencil or felt tip pen.

4 Clamp the rafters into place so that the feet are resting exactly onto the joins between opposite pairs of wall plates. Drill a 6mm hole in the foot of each rafter and screw them to the wall plates using 4in x 10g screws. These two initial rafters should be sufficient to hold the hexagonal centre post in place while the rest are fitted, but it may be found that three or four are required before the post is adequately supported.

5 Each time another rafter is added, use a tape measure to check that the distances from opposite corners of the wall plates to the hexagonal centre post are the same. Force the centre post upright and check it with a spirit level.

The purpose of Steps 2 to 5 is to hold the centre post in place so that the rafters can be cut to fit.

6 Cut another 3m length of 75 x 38mm timber in half to create two more rafters and place one half with its foot resting on the corner of the wall plate and its top resting on the centre post in such a way that its bottom corner touches the 30mm mark.

7 Use a spirit level to mark a vertical line on the end of the rafter touching the hexagonal centre post. Cut to this line and set the sliding bevel to this angle.

8 Rest the rafter into place with its cut end resting on the centre post and its top touching the 30mm mark. Use a spirit level to mark a horizontal line at the foot of the rafter where it rests on the joint between two wall plates. Cut to this line and rest the rafter in place.

9 Trim the top angle until the rafter is a good fit against both centre post and wall plate.

10 Rest the rafter in place and fix it to the centre post using a 2½in x 8g screw and to the wall plate using 3in x 10g screws.

11 The overhang can be sawn off or left.

12 Remove the pair of rafters used as the initial supports for the centre post and trim them to fit as set out in Steps 6 to 10. Cut the other four rafters to fit, using one of the trimmed rafters as a gauge. Screw the rafters to the hexagonal centre post using 2½in x 8g screws and to the wall plates using 3in x 10g screws. Check that the top of each rafter touches the 30mm line marked on the centre post.

The structure should now be self-supporting and quite rigid.

Cutting rafters with a birdsmouth

A birdsmouth cut at the foot of the rafter allows it to sit over the wall plate, but cutting a birdsmouth is quite complex. First decide if the corners of the wall plates are to be cut off or left in place.

1 To allow the birdsmouth to sit into and onto the area where the wall plates and the top of the post meet, the area where the wall plates join needs to be trimmed off. Use the sliding bevel to mark a cutting line on the corners, about 15mm along the joint between the wall plates.

2 Use a try square to mark a vertical cut on the sides of the wall plate.

3 Cut along these lines using a universal saw or tenon saw. The cut needs to go into the top of the temporary 75 x 75mm posts to a depth of 20mm to make room for the

feet of the rafters. To remove the triangle of wood from the top of the temporary post, cut across the corner of the post 20mm down from its top. Alternatively, the corners can be left uncut.

4 Cut the angle on the top of each rafter following Steps 2 to 5 on page 100. Once this has been done a birdsmouth can be cut at the foot of the rafter.

5 Clamp one pair of opposing rafters into place so that their feet are resting exactly on the join between opposing wall plates and their tops are resting on the hexagonal centre post. Check that the post is central by measuring between it and the corners of the wall plates. Use a spirit level to check that the centre post is upright.

6 Using 2½in x 8g screws, screw one rafter to the centre post with its top to the 30mm mark.

7 Use a spirit level to mark the horizontal cut required on the foot of the rafter. Parts of this line will form the foot of the birdsmouth.

8 Mark the position where the corners of the wall plates meet on the 38mm face at the foot of the rafter (or at the cut off corner).

9 Use a try square to draw a line at right angles across the timber so that it can be seen on the rafter's 75mm face.

10 Rest one side of a set square along the horizontal line drawn in Step 7 and the other side touching the point where the square line drawn in Steps 8 and 9 meets the 75mm face. Draw a line at this point (this is the plumb or vertical cut of the birdsmouth). Where the two cross will be the tip of the birdsmouth.

11 Use a try square to mark the birdsmouth's cut line on the 38mm face.

12 Mark the area to be cut out to form the birdsmouth.

13 The plumb (vertical) cut can be made using a universal hard point saw or a chop saw.

TIP *The chop saw may not penetrate to the full depth of the cut. If it doesn't the cut will need to be made using a universal hard point saw.*

14 The horizontal cut can be made using a universal hard point saw or a jigsaw.

TIP *If the corner between the horizontal and vertical cuts isn't clean use a universal hard point saw to remove the unwanted material.*

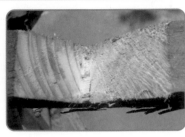

Follow the same procedure if the corners where the wall plates join on top of the posts have been cut back as in Steps 1 to 3.

15 Screw the foot of the birsmouthed rafter to the corner to verify that it fits and cut its bottom end to length. For our gazebo the rafter was finished with a vertical cut but more elaborate shapes could be applied to finish the rafter end.

16 Using the first rafter as a template cut the others in the same way. To ensure accuracy use the same rafter as a template every time.

In addition you should check the accuracy of the marks you make using the template by resting a sliding bevel set to the angle of the cut on the line and redrawing it. Do this for both the plumb cut and the horizontal cut.

17 Fix the remaining rafters in position.

Roof trellis

The design of the trellis is an opportunity to show your individuality and style. Using 38 x 18mm roofing battens as the supports for 38 x 10mm laths produces a robust trellis. The 38 x 10mm laths were cut from 75 x 38mm treated timber. The trellis can be screwed, nailed, pop-riveted or stapled together. See Chapter 1.

1 Use a circular saw or bench saw to cut the 38 x 10mm laths. If using a circular saw, set the blade to the correct depth (1mm or 2mm more than the thickness of the timber). To ensure that the timber is firmly secured while you work on it screw the timber onto two 38 x 75mm offcuts or similar and clamp or screw these to your workbench. See Chapter 1 for more details.

Use the guide built into the saw to ensure that the saw cuts 10mm wide laths.

TIP *Plan the location of the fixing holes for the work piece carefully so that the saw doesn't catch the screws.*

2 Temporarily nail a length of 38 x 10mm lath to the upper surface of the feet of one pair of rafters.

3 These laths will need to be cut at an angle where they meet on the rafter, but the angled ends don't need to be a snug fit. Set a sliding bevel to the angle required and mark this angle on both ends of the lath so that the cut is in the centre of the rafter. Pull the temporary nails out and cut the angle on both ends of the lath.

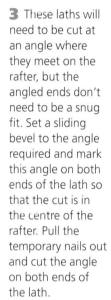

For easy reference, draw this angle onto another piece of wood and write on it what the angle is. The angle on the sliding bevel can be reset if necessary.

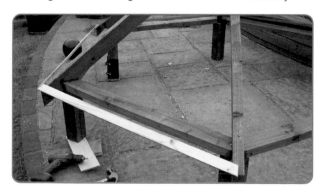

4 Having cut angles on the ends of all six bottom laths, use 1½in x 8g screws to screw the laths to the feet of the rafters. You should drill a 5mm hole for the screw but there's no need to countersink it.

5 To establish the locations of the remaining laths, measure the distance from the top of the bottom lath to the apex of the rafter and divide this up into equal-sized portions. For our gazebo these divisions worked out to 112mm (4¼in) from the top edge of one lath to the bottom edge of the lath above it. Temporarily nail the topmost lath in place 112mm from

the hexagonal centre post, making sure as you do so that it's parallel with the bottom lath.

6 Use 50mm nails to temporarily nail in place all the laths on one side, making sure that they're parallel with the bottom lath. The ends of the laths do not need to be cut to size yet. Don't drive

the nails in too far – leave enough protruding to allow them to be pulled out using a claw hammer.

7 Mark the centres of the top and bottom laths. Also make marks a quarter of the way and three-quarters of the way along the bottom lath.

8 Cut a piece of 38 x 18mm roofing batten so that it fits under the laths into the apex between the two rafters and reaches to the bottom of the bottom lath (on our gazebo this measured 1m). Make a mark 50mm from one end of this batten (which now becomes its top). Slip the batten under the top and bottom laths and clamp it into place so that it's positioned behind the centre marks you made on the top and bottom laths. Its top should overlap the top lath by the 50mm you marked.

9 Cut two more support battens the same length and clamp them into place so that their tops wedge between the centre batten and the rafters. The bottoms of these battens should rest behind the quarter-length and three-quarter-length marks on the bottom lath.

10 Mark these three battens along the bottom edge of the bottom lath and cut them to length.

11 Replace the battens and screw through the laths into them. Drill a 4mm hole for the 1in x 6g screws.

12 Fix the other laths into place – there's no need to cut them to length.

13 Use a straight edge as a guide to mark the cutting lines at both ends of each lath. This line needs to be marked so that the cuts are along the centreline of each rafter.

14 Remove the temporary nails securing the laths onto the rafters. Undo the screws holding the bottom lath and lift the entire trellis panel out. Rest it on a steady surface and cut off the excess lath ends.

15 Replace the panel, securing it with the two bottom screws.

16 Construct the other five trellis panels in the same way, with the spaces between the laths accurately matching those on the first one. The angles you cut at the lath ends will need to match those on the adjacent panels, and on the final panel the angles will have to be cut at both ends as the laths are fitted into place.

 *Label the trellis panels so that they go back in the same places – use small labels or a felt-tip pen.*

17 Before all the trellis panels are put in, you need to fix the finial to the top of the hexagonal centre post if one is going to be fitted. The base provided with the finial was cut to form a hexagon. Then drill a 6mm hole in the centre of the top of the post and screw in the dowel screw provided with the finial, using a pair of pliers if necessary. Screw the finial onto the dowel screw.

18 Treat the entire trellis thoroughly and allow to dry.

Post fixing

Once the roof has been assembled at ground level it can be dismantled, making it easier to reassemble on top of the full-height posts. Remove the trellis, the rafters and the hexagonal support post, making sure that you label them first for identification purposes. Leave intact the basic hexagonal framework of the wall plates screwed to the 300mm lengths of 75 x 75mm fence post.

Though the posts could be concreted directly into the ground, setting them into a spur not only makes it easier to replace them if they should rot, but helps prevent rot by keeping the posts out of direct contact with the ground. Our gazebo used Metpost spurs.

Rapid set (post fix) concrete is available which can be used to secure the posts or spurs in the ground.

The most difficult aspect of fixing the posts is getting the spurs into the ground in the correct place, at the correct angle, and upright.

1 Set the basic hexagonal framework of the gazebo into place and mark the exact location of one of the posts. Peg a length of timber in place to show the angle at which the post or post spur needs to be set. Getting the tops of

the spurs level makes it easier when it comes to fixing the trellis or sides. However, it isn't necessary for all the post spurs to be at the same level in the ground – the posts themselves can be cut to different lengths to level them at the top.

TIP *If the ground isn't level start with the post at the highest point. The other posts can be set a little higher to compensate for the slope so that the tops are level.*

2 Drive the post spur into the ground using a dolly and a large lump hammer or a sledge hammer. As it's driven in, check that it's upright and aligned with the guide timber. Make up a 'twister' to turn the spur if necessary – a length of timber screwed to a spare bolt-down plate or a short length of post is ideal.

4 Stand the gazebo roof frame (still on its short legs) with one leg in the post spur and align it so that the location of the next spur can be marked and the spur driven in. Mark this location as accurately as possible – any slight deviation will set the posts off vertical. Check that the spur is at the right angle as you drive it in. Fix the other four posts, following the procedures above if spurs are being used.

5 Of its six spurs, our gazebo had three driven directly into the ground, one which needed to be concreted into place, and two bolt-down types to allow for adjustment. If you have problems driving the spurs into the ground accurately it's a good idea to cast concrete pads and use bolt-down spurs.

TIP *If you need to move a spur it can be lifted out of the ground by making up a lever that fits under its cup and rests on a fulcrum.*

3 Drive the post in until it's the required level, checking as you do so that it's upright in both directions. Take care regarding the location of the bolts – they need to be as inconspicuous as possible. If necessary check to ensure that the spurs are level.

To set a spur in concrete, first dig a small hole for the spur and the concrete. Place the spur in the hole and pour some concrete in around it. Then position and align the spur, check it's level with the spurs already fitted and check that it's upright using a spirit level – ideally one with a built-in magnet – before the concrete begins to cure. When the

spur has been accurately located, pour the remainder of the mix of 4:1 gravel/cement into the hole to hold the spur in place.

If possible replace the frame to check that the spurs are aligned correctly and are the correct level before all the concrete is added, and check again before it sets. When the concrete has had a chance to set (a day should be enough) the posts can be pushed into the spurs.

For bolt-down spurs, cast a concrete pad about 200mm thick and twice the size of the plate of the spur. Check that the pad is level using a spirit level (rest the spirit level on your trowel to avoid getting it covered in concrete). If the pad needs to be above ground, either build shuttering to the correct level or set part of a paving slab on top of the concrete. The spur should not be fixed in place yet, in order that its location can be adjusted once the frame is in place (see Step 11 below).

6 Decide on the height of the wall plate – for our gazebo this was 1880mm (74in). Mark this height on one post and cut it to length. Ensure the treated end of the timber is at the bottom and cut one end only.

7 Set the cut post into the spur. If the spurs are at the same level all the posts can be cut to the same length. If the spurs aren't level with each other, set the posts into

their sockets and use a straight edge and a long spirit level to determine the correct height for each. Mark these levels and add an identification mark so that you know which post belongs in which spur. Cut all the posts to length.

To mark the height of the posts in the bolt-down spurs rest the post into the spur and, with someone holding it upright, mark the height. In fact it's better if someone can hold each of the posts upright while the measurements are being made. However, as long as a post is about upright the measurement will be accurate enough.

Safety If using a ladder to reach the tops of the posts make sure it's positioned well and that the feet are resting on something firm and level.

TIP *If the posts are cut too short by mistake they can be rested on something (slate, lead, tile – anything thing that doesn't rot) placed in the spur to build up their height.*

8 When the posts have been cut, draw a diagonal on the cut (top) end of each. Mark the notch that needs to be cut out (if any) for the foot of the rafter to sit into. This can be measured off the temporary 300mm posts. For our gazebo this was 20mm down from the top and 15mm along the diagonal from the corner. Set a sliding bevel to the angle on the short posts and mark this onto the end of the post.

9 Use a universal hard point saw to cut along these lines to create the notch. Do this on each of the six posts.

Before the wall plates are removed from the short posts, make identification marks on the plates so that they can be relocated in the same places.

10 Unscrew one wall plate from the temporary posts and rest it in place on top of the new full-height posts. Align it with the diagonal and screw it into place using the original 3in x 10g screw. Fix all the wall plates in the same way and check that the posts are upright.

TIP *If the posts aren't upright they can be pushed into place and supported there using timber braces.*

11 When the posts have all been forced into an upright position fix any bolt-down plates – two in the case of our gazebo. Use rawl bolts or suitable-sized plugs.

12 The bolt-down plates for our gazebo were secured using 1½in x 5mm coach screws set into washers. The plugs needed a 10mm hole in the concrete, which was drilled using a

10mm masonry bit and a mains-powered drill. It's very important to use the correct size drill bit for the plug and the correct size plug for the screw/bolt. Tighten all the bolts holding the bolt-down plates in place.

Safety Always ensure that any mains-powered tools are protected by an RCD (trip). *Do not use them in wet conditions.*

13 Ensure the posts are upright and tighten the bolts that grip the posts.

Fitting the roof

When all the wall plates have been fixed and the posts have been secured the roof can be fitted. If you have access to a tower scaffold this makes the job easier and safer. If not work off one or two step ladders making sure they are safe.

1 Screw the feet of two rafters to the wall plates at the location that was marked when the roof was originally assembled. On our gazebo 5in x 12g yellowed zinc screws were used – the screws went into the top of the post, not just into the wall plates.

2 Once the foot of each rafter has been secured, screw the tops of the rafters to the correct location on the hexagonal centre post. Replace the 2½in x 8g screws with 63mm deck screws.

Assemble the rest of the rafters in the same way. It may be necessary to force them into place either at the wall plates or the centre post. While doing this make sure that the tops of the rafters align with the 30mm line and that the feet of the rafters are pushed right into the notch in the top of each post. When this has been done the roof of the gazebo should be quite sturdy.

3 Fix each trellis roof panel to the same segment of the roof as before. Drill a 5mm hole and use 1½in screws to fix the top lath of the trellis to the top of the rafters and the bottom lath to their feet. Though it probably won't be necessary to fix the trellis more securely it can also be screwed or nailed through the other laths if you so desire.

The trellis sides

The top of each gazebo side trellis was set about 900mm above ground level, this height being chosen because it looked right. It may pay to sit in the area to assess what height best suits your own preferences. Consider what the gazebo is to be used for: is it for sitting in, or is it a bower over which to grow plants? If the latter, you may want the trellises to run from top to bottom to help support climbing plants. If not, you may decide to have no side trellises at all.

If constructing trellises isn't in your repertoire buy pre-made trellises and fit them into place.

Fitting a support for the trellis/handrail

The top rail to which the trellis is to be fixed is made from 75 x 38mm treated timber with a separate strip of 38 x 19mm roofing batten added to cover the top of the trellis. The top rail was sanded after it had been fitted but it could have been sanded first.

The bottom rail was cut in the same way as the top rail and was fitted so that it rested on the tops of the spurs. If the spurs are set level this is easy. If they weren't, align the bottom rails so that they're level all round, otherwise the trellis will look lopsided. This alignment will need to be taken from the highest spur.

1 To mark the correct angle on the bottom rail, cut a length of 75 x 38mm about 20mm longer than the greatest distance between the uprights (posts) it's being fitted between. Hold this into place on the inside of the uprights, just a little above the top of the spurs. Use a combination square to mark the exact location of the corners of the posts. (A combination square was used because the length could be adjusted to rest at the corner of the post so that the corner mark could be made on the rail where it touched the post.)

2 Still holding the rail in place, set a sliding bevel to the correct angle at one end.

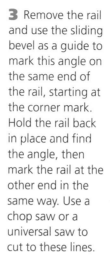

3 Remove the rail and use the sliding bevel as a guide to mark this angle on the same end of the rail, starting at the corner mark. Hold the rail back in place and find the angle, then mark the rail at the other end in the same way. Use a chop saw or a universal saw to cut to these lines.

> **TIP** *If you're using a chop saw, cut the rail a little longer and try it to see if it fits. It can then be judged if the angle of cut was accurate. If it wasn't, adjust the angle of the saw and cut off a little more.*

4 When the bottom rail fits do the same with the top rail, holding it at the height mark. Don't assume that they'll be the same length as the bottom rail, though the angles will be the same. When it's cut to length, push the top rail into place so that the edges are aligned with the corners of the uprights. Drill a 5mm hole in the end of the top rail so that a screw will go into the upright. Drive in a 63mm screw to hold one end in place. Level the top rail and drill and fix the other end in the same way.

Cut and fix the top and bottom rails in the same way in each section that's to have a trellis. Check that the bottom rails are level and that all the top rails line up around the gazebo.

5 When all the top rails have been fixed, a length of 38 x 18mm batten can be added to the outside of the top rail to cover the top of each trellis; this is called a trellis cap. Cut it to the same length as the outside of the top rail.

the 18mm face of each batten and screw them into place on the 38mm outside face of the top rail, using 63mm deck screws.

Mark the 18mm thickness of the batten onto the 38mm face. From this mark, use a sliding bevel set at a suitable angle (in this case 30°) to mark angles on the ends of each trellis cap and cut to these lines.

The trellis battens

6 When the angles have been cut drill three 5mm holes in

7 Cut five lengths of batten to act as vertical supports for each panel of trellis, so that they sit under the trellis cap fixed to the top rail and end just clear the ground. Mark the location of these

battens. The two outermost ones are set a batten's width from the posts with the other three spaced out between them. Take care that the battens are parallel and equally spaced.

8 Drill 5mm holes in the battens to coincide with the top and bottom support rails. Then screw all the battens in place to the top and bottom rails, using 63mm deck screws.

TIP *It will be necessary to angle the 5mm holes in the tops of the battens so that the screws will go into the top rail without splitting it.*

9 Sand the top rails to give a smooth finish and remove splinters before treating the timber.

10 When the vertical battens have been fixed, cut the horizontal laths as suggested in Step 1 of the roof trellis construction (page 105). Clamp these into place initially to establish the best location for them. On our gazebo the top and bottom laths were set a lath's width down from the top rail and up from the bottom rail.

11 These battens can be screwed into place using 1in x 6g screws, can be pop riveted, or can be glued. It was found that screwing the ends of the battens and gluing the other joints worked well if the trellis was flat but if it was vertical the glue ran down the uprights.

12 When fixing the horizontal laths on adjacent bays use a try square to mark lines around the post to ensure that the battens in both bays line up.

Depending on the distance between the ground and the bottom rail, laths of batten can be fitted at this level in the same way.

13 Treat the gazebo with a good quality timber preservative.

Building a pergola

Because the pergola described here was built onto the decking constructed in Chapter 3 its uprights were bolted to the joists of the decking. However, one built to stand on the ground would have its posts fixed as described for the gazebo.

Plan the base area carefully and decide how the surface or the ground will be finished. If paving slabs are to be laid, ensure that the posts of the pergola are suitable distances apart. If it's to be on the lawn, be certain that your mower will go between the posts. In other words plan the job carefully and check that the pergola is an appropriate size.

A sloping site presents no problems but it's necessary to decide on the minimum height of the crosspieces. This is dictated by the height of the longitudinal pieces that they rest on. Start with this height at the top of the slope – that way the headroom under the crosspieces increases as the structure is built down the slope. It's far better if the longitudinal pieces are level, but they can be stepped to accommodate steep slopes.

Though the removal of existing decking planks and the like is not covered here the work involved in replacing it is described.

The pergola described is 2.85m long and 2m high to the underside of the crosspieces. The posts are of 100 x 100mm treated timber sanded to a smoother finish with the corners (arrises) sanded to a more rounded form. However, this wasn't an essential part of the construction process and the posts can be left in their raw state if you prefer.

It was decided that the 89 x 38mm longitudinal pieces should be a little below the level of the guttering of the conservatory. This meant that the 89 x 38mm crosspieces were also below the gutter.

Materials
- 6 2.4m lengths of 100 x 100mm treated timber for posts
- 10 3m lengths of 89 x 38mm treated timber for the longitudinal pieces and crosspieces
- 6 M10 x 100mm bolts
- 6 M10 x 150mm Bolts
- 12 10mm nuts
- 24 10mm washers
- Timber treatment
- 16 10mm dowels for filling crosspiece screw holes
- Waterproof adhesive
- 16 4in x 8g screws
- 63mm deck screws (quantity will depend on amount of decking to be fixed)
- Post spurs (quantity will depend on how many posts are being erected)
- Post concrete

Tools
- Universal hard point saw
- Tenon saw
- Chop saw
- Jigsaw
- Extension lead
- RCD (or safety plug)
- Belt sander
- Twist drill bits
  15mm flat or twist
  6mm
- Screw sink and plug cutter
- Flat drill bits
  15mm
  10mm
- Screwdriver bits
  Square No 2
  Posi (PZ) No 2
- Hammer
- Workbench
- Clamps
- Spirit level long
- Try square
- Combination square
- Pencil
- Tape measure
- Sliding bevel
- 13mm spanner
- Adjustable spanner
- 25mm (1in) chisel
- Mallet
- Safety glasses
- Dust mask
- Gloves
- Ear defenders

The posts

The posts at the front were cut out (rebated) to allow them to fit over the front joist of the decking, but the back (inner) posts didn't need rebating – they bolted directly to the joists. Choose the most attractive pieces of timber for the front or outer posts since they're the ones that will be in full view.

1 Cut a rebate out of the base of the three front posts. The rebates in these posts were all cut to the same length (200mm) and trimmed to fit later. 40mm of timber was left in place to accommodate the thickness of the skirting and allow a 15mm overlap in front of it. The 60mm cut-out was to fit over the joist.

To cut the rebate, first make a mark 200mm from the base of the post and draw a line around the post at this point, using a try square as a guide. Draw a line from the 200mm mark to the base. This is 40mm in from one face. Do the same on the opposite face. Use a try square to draw a line on the base of the post connecting the two 40mm lines. Then mark the section of timber to be removed – otherwise it's all too easy to cut out the wrong section!

This is exactly the same operation as was followed to cut the rebates on the decking newel posts in Chapter 3 (page 83, Steps 5 and 6).

> **TIP** *Start sawing slowly and ensure that the saw is cutting along both 40mm lines and the line at the end of the post. When the saw reaches the 200mm line, turn the post over and cut from the other side. This should help to ensure that the saw stays on the lines.*

2 Sand the posts to remove rough areas, splinters and any pencil marks. Use the sander to round off the corners. Treat the cut areas with a suitable timber treatment. We opted for a clear treatment because the pergola wasn't going to be colour treated for a year or so.

Safety Put the tin, and any container used for the treatment, well out of the way of children and pets.

3 Each front post has the same depth rebate cut into it, but in some cases the rebate may need to be shortened a little. To check this, use a combination square to find the depth of the joist at the location of each post.

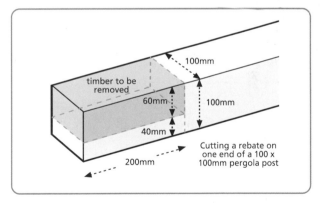

timber to be removed

100mm

60mm

100mm

40mm

200mm

Cutting a rebate on one end of a 100 x 100mm pergola post

4 Transfer this depth to the rebate of the post to be used.

5 Use a try square to mark this line all around the bottom of the post.

6 Cut the post to length along this line and treat the cut end.

7 Clamp a front post which has been cut to length into place against the joist and check that it's upright. For safety you should have a helper to hold the post while you do this. When the post is upright drill a 10mm bolt hole through it and the joist – a 10mm flat bit will be long enough to go through both. This hole should be about 25mm in from one edge and 25mm up from the bottom of the post – you need to leave sufficient room for a second hole to be added in Step 10.

8 The front posts were bolted to the joist using M10 (10mm) x 100mm bolts. A washer should be fitted under the head of the bolt and under the nut.

9 The bolts on the front posts were driven in from the front so that the heads are seen, not the nuts. Fit the washer and tighten the nut using a 13mm spanner.

TIP *Two spanners may be need, the second one (an adjustable spanner would be ideal) being to hold the head of the bolt to stop it rotating.*

10 Check that the post is upright, prop it in place and remove the clamp. Drill a second 10mm hole about 25mm down from the top of the rebate and 25mm in from the edge, drive the bolt in and tighten the nut – checking as you do so that the post is still upright. It will be possible to push the post so that it's upright along the line of the joist, but if the joist is twisted the post won't stay upright in the other direction. This can be rectified later when the decking boards are fixed.

11 Fix the other two front posts in the same way, using at least two bolts per post. The bolts on the end posts were set one above the other because they were near the ends of the front joist. Check all three are upright and that the bolts are tight.

12 Next bolt the three back posts to the decking joists. To do this, measure along the joists in order to locate the posts the same distance from one end as the front ones. Clamp one post in place, check it's upright, drill a 10mm hole about 25mm down from the top of the joist and 25mm in from the edge of the post, and fit a bolt. Tighten the nut, remove the clamp and drill a hole for the second bolt about 25mm up from the bottom of the post and 25mm in from the edge of the post. Keep checking that the post is upright. Drive in the bolt and do up all the nuts.

Fitting the longitudinal pieces

Decide on which side of the post the 89 x 38mm longitudinal pieces will be fixed, and the amount by which they'll overlap the posts at each end of the pergola. This can be calculated from the bottom of the posts, since if they're upright they'll be the same distance apart at the top and bottom of the posts.

1 Decide how the ends of the longitudinal and crosspieces will be cut. The cuts used on the pergola were made using a chop saw.

2 Curved ends can be cut using a jigsaw. Mark the curve using a paint tin or similar circular object and then cut it using a jigsaw.

3 Once all the posts have been bolted into place and you've checked that they're upright, clamp a longitudinal

piece into place along the top of the posts so that it overlaps them by the same amount at each end. Make sure that the longitudinal piece is level. Mark the position of the bottom of the longitudinal piece on each of the posts, and the position of the posts at each end of the longitudinal piece. For obvious safety reasons this is a two-person job!

4 Drill a 5mm hole in each end of the longitudinal piece and screw it into place using a 63mm deck screw. This is a temporary fixing. Screw the other end of the longitudinal piece into place against the second post.

5 Fix the opposite longitudinal piece in the same way. Check across the two pieces to ensure that they're level with each other.

6 On our pergola the longitudinal pieces were rebated into the tops of the posts. However, this isn't necessary: the longitudinal pieces can be simply bolted to the posts instead, using M10 (10mm) x 150mm bolts. To do this, follow Steps 3 to 5 above. Drill a 10mm hole, 25mm down from the top of the longitudinal piece and 25mm in from one edge of the post. Fit the bolt, with washers, and tighten the nut. Do the same on each post. Drill another bolt hole at each post about 25mm up from the bottom of the longitudinal piece and 25mm in from the opposite edge of the upright. The temporary screw can be left in place or removed.

If you opt for rebates, first mark the tops and bottoms of the longitudinal pieces on all the posts, checking that they're upright before this is done. Then remove the longitudinal pieces and one row of posts.

Use a try square to mark the lines more clearly.

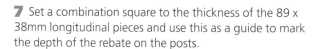

10 Use a try square to mark a line on the end of the post from the cut line marked with the combination square. Carefully saw along this line to remove the rebate. Cut the rebates on the three posts, treat the cut areas, and replace the posts.

7 Set a combination square to the thickness of the 89 x 38mm longitudinal pieces and use this as a guide to mark the depth of the rebate on the posts.

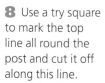

8 Use a try square to mark the top line all round the post and cut it off along this line.

9 Cut across the timber to the depth of the rebate, taking care to cut the correct side of the line.

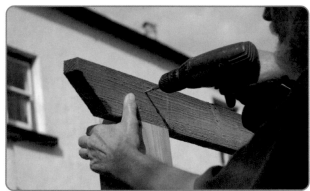

11 Check that the replaced posts are upright. Rest the longitudinal piece in place and check that it overlaps by the same amount at each end. Drill a 6mm hole in it where it meets each post and drive a 63mm deck screw into each. Check that the posts are upright as each screw is driven in.

12 Repeat the entire process with the posts and longitudinal piece on the other side of the pergola.

Fitting the crosspieces

The crosspieces for our pergola were notched to allow them to fit over the longitudinal pieces, but this isn't necessary: they could be simply rested on top and screwed into place using 4in screws. To do this, drill a 30mm-deep 10mm counterbore hole to recess the head of the screw by the required amount. This hole can be filled with dowelling after the crosspieces have been fixed.

1 Cut one 38 x 89mm crosspiece to a length sufficient to overlap the longitudinal pieces by the required amount. Rest it on top of the longitudinal pieces and check that it fits and looks alright. Decide on how many crosspieces are needed – this is very much a matter of personal preference. The two crosspieces on our pergola, one on either side of the centre post, were a design decision, not a structural one.

2 Cut all the crosspieces to length and shape the ends.

3 Lay the first crosspiece at the base of the posts and mark the position of the outside edge of the post on it at each end. This will be the same distance as the outside edges of the longitudinal pieces. Using the bottom of the posts as a guide when marking the crosspieces means that they tend to pull the posts upright when they're fitted to the longitudinal pieces.

4 Use an offcut of 89 x 38mm timber to mark the width of the notch in the crosspieces so that they fit over the longitudinal pieces. Don't make the notches a tight fit: it's necessary to allow for expansion of the wood when it gets wet.

5 Use a try square to mark the sides of the notch and a combination square, set to 30mm, to mark the depth.

6 Saw down the two sides of the cut and use a mallet and chisel to remove the timber from the notch. Clean up the base of the notch and, using an offcut, check that it will fit over the longitudinal piece.

for the two side cuts of the notch, the back section would still have to be cut out with a chisel or a jigsaw.

TIP *Don't try to remove all the timber in one go – remove half, then turn the wood over and remove the remainder.*

8 Cut both notches and check that the cut crosspiece fits onto the longitudinal pieces. Note that if the posts aren't upright the crosspiece won't fit. If necessary, prop the posts upright before checking the fit.

Mark and cut out the notches on the other crosspieces using the first one as a template. Treat the cut timber.

9 Prop the posts upright.

7 Alternatively drill a 15mm hole in the notch area to allow a jigsaw blade to enter and then saw along the back line of the notch.

Though a chop saw could be set to the correct depth

Decking and balustrade

1 If the pergola is being built into a deck, the decking boards and skirting will need to be fitted once the pergola has been completed. To install the decking follow the instructions given in Chapter 3.

10 Drill a 6mm hole in the centre of each notch and counterbore it with a 10mm drill bit so that a 63mm deck screw penetrates about 30mm into the notch. Rest the crosspieces into their correct places and drive in the deck screws.

11 Glue a length of 10mm dowel into each counterbore hole to stop water from getting in. When the glue is dry cut the excess off using a tenon saw.

2 With a deck the pergola can be considered a completed structure – whether or not a balustrade is fitted is a matter of choice, but if you decide to add one follow the instructions given in Chapter 3.

BUILDING A SHED

Materials

The following is a list of the materials you may need; it is not a cutting list. Make an individual list for the shed you're going to build. All measurements given are for the shed built in this chapter.

Quantity	Materials	Purpose
Sawn and treated timber		
1	2.4m length 100 x 50mm (4 x 2in) treated timber (need not be treated)	Ridge purlin
6	1.9m lengths 75 x 50mm (3 x 2in) treated timber	Floor joists
6	3.6m lengths 75 x 50m (3 x 2in) treated timber (need not be treated)	Rafters
30	3.6m lengths 50 x 25mm (2 x 1in) treated roofing batten	Side frames; end frames; 'A' frame collars; door head; window opening; cladding supports; packing pieces; corner pieces for cladding; roofing support; roof eaves
Planed square edge timber (PSE)		
1	2.1m length	Door ledges
1	4.2m length	
1	3.6m length	Uprights for door frame
1	– 75 x 25mm (3 x 1in) PSE (finished size 69 x 20mm)	Head (top) of the door frame; window frame
1	4m length parting bead or plain moulding, about 20 x 8mm	Beading for glass
3	2.4m lengths 120 x 18mm tongued-and-grooved V-jointed (TGV) timber	Door
1	1m Scotia	
Sheet material		
2 sheets	18 x 2440 x 1220mm (8 x 4ft) plywood	Floor

Quantity	Fixing (all screws to be BZP)	Purpose
20	3in x 8g screws	Apex battens and fixing 'A' frames
Box	63mm deck screws (FastenMaster)	For general fixing
Box	2½in x 8g screws	Alternative to FastenMaster
Box	1½in x 8g screws	Miscellaneous fixings
Box	1¼in x 8g screws	Door ledge etc
2	10in or 12in 'T' hinges galvanised	Door
1	Galvanised turn button	Door fastening
16	4in x 8g screws	To fix apex batten for OSB roof decking
0.5kg	30mm (1¼in) galvanised clout nails	Top of feather-edge
0.5kg	38mm (1½in) galvanised oval nails	Bottom of feather-edge or shiplap
50	50mm (2in) galvanised lost head nails	Fixing bargeboard

Quantity	Miscellaneous	Purpose
0.5kg	1½in galvanised oval nails	Fixing shingles
0.5kg	2in galvanised lost head nails	Fixing battens
0.5kg	13mm galvanised clout nails	Roofing felt
Box	1in x 8g screws	Top of feather-edge if not nailed
Box	2¼in x 8g screws	Fixing shiplap

Quantity	OSB and felt roof system	Purpose
3	12mm x 1220 x 2440mm sheets Oriented Strand Board OSB	Roofing sheets (not needed on shingle roof)
1	4.6m length 75 x 25mm (3 x 1in) PSE	Bargeboard
1 roll	Shed roofing felt	
1 litre	Aqua Seal felt adhesive	

Quantity	Feather-edge cladding	Purpose
60	2.4m lengths Ex 125 x 22mm feather-edge	Cladding shed
5 litre tin	Timber treatment	Timber preservation

Shiplap cladding

25	4.2m lengths 19 x 125mm shiplap	Cladding shed
2	2m lengths 22m quadrant	Glass beading for window (shiplap shed)
1	1m length 22mm Scotia	Drip above door (shiplap shed)

Miscellaneous

	Adhesive (exterior)	
	Exterior paint (Sadolin Superdeck Jungle Green)	
	Glass or perspex to fit	Window

Cedar shingle roof

2 packets	Cedar shingles	Roof
1 packet	Cedar ridges	Roof ridge
10	3.6m lengths 50 x 25mm (2 x 1in) treated roofing batten	Roof

Planed square edge timber (PSE)

2	4.6m lengths 125 x 25mm (5 x 1in) PSE	Bargeboards

Tools

- Universal hard point saw
- Chop saw
- Circular saw
- Jigsaw
- Extension lead
- RCD (or safety plug)
- Belt sander/power sander
- Electric planer or hand plane
- Mains-powered electric drill with hammer action
- Screwdriver or cordless drill/driver
- Twist drill bits
  5mm
  4mm
  2mm
- Countersink bit
- Screwdriver bits
  Posi (PZ) No 2
  Square No 2
- Posi (PZ) No 2 hand-powered

- Hammer
- Workbench
- Clamps
- Spirit level (long)
- Try square
- Combination square
- Pencil
- Tape measure
- Chalk or chalk line
- Builders' line
- Sliding bevel
- Straight edge (long spirit level is ideal)
- 25mm (1in) chisel
- Mallet
- Rubber mallet
- Brush for adhesive
- Pliers – long nose
- Retractable trimming knife
- Scissors
- Scaffold
- Step ladders
- Safety glasses
- Dust mask
- Ear defenders
- Gloves

Sheds that can be bought from garden centres and DIY stores are good value for money and I would be surprised if you could build one for less. However, they do have some disadvantages, an obvious one being that they come in set sizes. If you need a shed to fit a certain space or for a particular purpose, you'll need to build it yourself or have it made for you.

The design of a shed is another consideration. You can go anywhere in the country and see the same off-the-shelf sheds. These are all the same shape with the same cladding in the same colour and the same roof style: utilitarian but not attractive. They show no local variations in cladding, no alteration of roof pitch to suit the local design, no variation in roofing material and, worst of all to my mind, no individual foibles. I've designed the shed in this chapter so that it can be built to express some originality and individuality.

The construction methods described allow the shed to be built using different cladding and roofing. In addition the size of the shed and the pitch of the roof can be altered to suit the owner's requirements and the shed's surroundings. The framework can be made to any size (within reason) and clad using a wide range of materials which could include corrugated iron, waney-edged timber (with bark still on the edges), vertical boarding, rendering, mock Tudor half-timber, and so on. In addition, the choice of roofing material is flexible.

I feel sure that you're embarking on the building of a shed in order to achieve an individualised, tailor-made structure. If this is the case, take into consideration the pitch of the roofs of local buildings, always a good indicator of a local style. Remember, a steep pitch to the roof may increase the overall height of the shed and take it

over 4m. If so it will then need Planning Permission – a requirement to be avoided if at all possible!

The instructions given in this chapter are for a shed which is 1880mm (74in) wide and 2035mm (80in) long, with a roof pitch of 35°. It's a simple matter to make the shed longer, but making it wider may involve altering the roof pitch or height.

One advantage of building your own shed is being able to construct one suited to your requirements – that is, it can be built with the windows and doors placed to suit your needs (whatever they are); to fit the space available; to complement its surroundings; and to give you the space you require. Draw a floorplan to make sure that the stuff you want in the shed will fit. Check that the bench will fit under the window and allow the door to open; check that the lawnmower, wheelbarrow, motorcycle, piano, or whatever else needs to go in through the door will do so. While you're at this planning stage also ensure that your plans don't run foul of any regulations.

See Chapter 1 for more details on planning.

Structural considerations

The shed must stand on a firm base – not earth or grass. Concrete, firmly laid paving slabs or well-compacted scalpings (sub-base or hogging) or gravel would be ideal. Failing this set the main 75 x 50mm (3 x 2in) treated timber joists onto bricks or blocks so that each floor joist is supported every 400mm (16in).

The dimensions given are for the shed built in this chapter. Please check your own measurements and don't rely on the ones given. The imperial and metric conversions aren't accurate: they're only close approximations. If you need accurate conversions consult an imperial-metric conversion table.

Make sure you have the space to build the shed. Ours was built in a 9 x 20ft (2.75 x 6.1m) garage, but it was a tight fit. You need a solid, easy to clean base to work on. To achieve this the concrete floor in the garage was painted so that it was dust free and easy to sweep after any work was done. However, headroom may be a problem: you'll be very lucky indeed if you can fully assemble the shed inside your workspace, wherever it is.

Each aspect of the project involves simple methods of construction. There are no complex joints or difficult cuts. However, angles do need to be cut as accurately as possible – a good quality chop saw will make this easier.

One general rule of thumb you may find helpful is to always cut a length of timber 50mm longer than is required. Hold it in place, mark the correct length and *then* make the cut. This cut long / hold in place / mark / cut / fit approach can be a lot more accurate than working by measurement.

Constructing the base (floor)

The base is 1880mm (74in) wide x 2035mm (80in) long. Its 1880mm 75 x 50mm joists run from side to side. The 75 x 50mm floor joists will provide adequate support for a shed constructed on a solid area (oversite) such as paving slabs, concrete or compacted gravel.

The base needs to be built first so that it can be used as a firm surface to work on and to use as a check for the sizes of the roof 'A' frames, the end frames and the side frames.

1 Cut six 1880mm 75 x 50mm floor joists. Soak the cut ends in timber treatment for ten minutes or the time recommended on the tin.

2 Cut the floor to size from two 2440 x 1220mm (8 x 4ft) sheets of 18mm plywood. Sheet 1 needs to be cut to 1220 x 2035mm (48 x 80in), Sheet 2 needs to be 2035 x 660mm (26 x 80in). Keep the offcuts – they'll be used later.

Safety When cutting the plywood sheets ensure they're secure and won't move while being worked on. See Chapter 1 for methods of cutting plywood. Alternatively, ask the supplier to cut it for you.

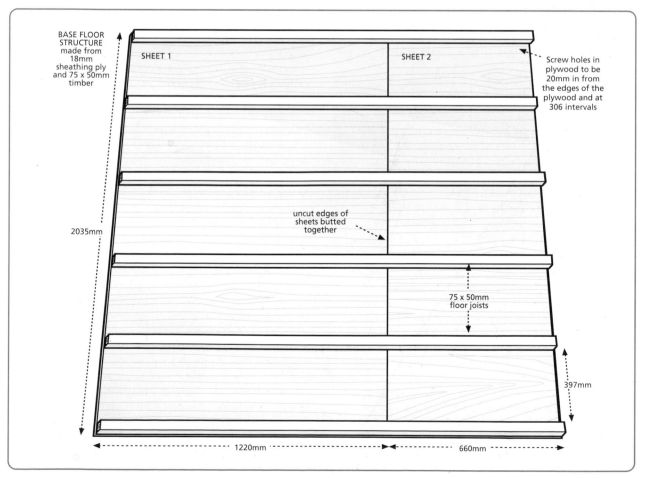

BASE FLOOR STRUCTURE made from 18mm sheathing ply and 75 x 50mm timber

SHEET 1

SHEET 2

Screw holes in plywood to be 20mm in from the edges of the plywood and at 306 intervals

2035mm

uncut edges of sheets butted together

75 x 50mm floor joists

397mm

1220mm

660mm

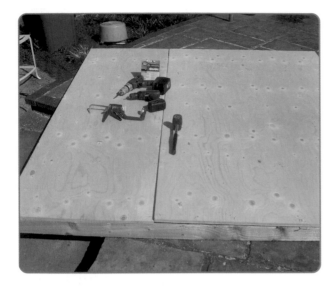

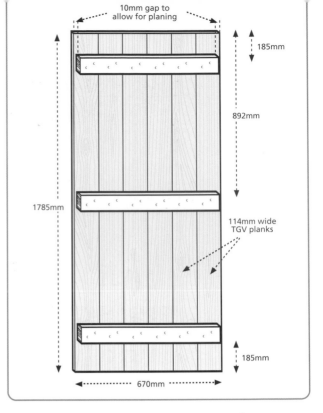

10mm gap to allow for planing

185mm

892mm

1785mm

114mm wide TGV planks

185mm

670mm

3 Lay the two cut sheets on a flat surface, with their uncut 2035mm sides together, and mark the position of the centre of each joist along each 2035mm edge. (See main plan.) On our shed the centres of these joists were 397mm apart.

Draw a line between these marks to indicate the centre line of each joist.

Drill and countersink a series of 5mm holes for the 63mm deck screws. These holes should be 20mm in from the edges of the plywood and 306mm apart.

4 Lay the two end joists on a flat surface and rest plywood Sheet 1 on top of them so that they line up exactly with the edges of the plywood and with the centre lines marked in Step 3. If possible clamp these joists into place and screw the plywood to them. Otherwise align them as accurately as possible and screw just one end, then align and screw the other end. Slide the four remaining joists under the plywood base so that the centre of the end of each joist aligns with the centre marks on the plywood.

Lay the second piece of plywood in place then mark and fix it in the same way. Take care that Sheet 1 and Sheet 2 are touching along their length. Drive in all the screws, then treat all cut ends or edges, both sides of the plywood and the joists.

Safety The completed base is robust and quite heavy, and it's a two-person job to lift and move it.

Constructing the door

The door of our shed measures 673 x 1785mm (26½ x 70½in). The width of the door will, to some extent, be dictated by the width of the planks from which it's made, and if it was constructed before the shed it could be made to the size of the planks and need not be trimmed to fit a door opening. Ours was built using tongued-and-grooved V-jointed planks (TGV or PTGV) with a face cover of 114mm (4½in) and a thickness of 16mm, six of which produced a width of 673mm (26½in) after the tongue of one plank and the groove of another had been removed.

1 Cut the 120 x 18mm TGV into 1785mm lengths using a chop saw or universal/hard point saw.

2 Fix one length into a workbench and plane off the tongue. Fix another length into the workbench and plane off the groove. The tongue and groove can be planed off using a power or hand plane. Try to remove the same amount of timber from each so that the planks at each side of the door are the same width.

Safety Make sure the planks are well secured while planing them.

3 Decide on the surface you'll be working on – it needs to be flat. Two workbenches, with plywood clamped in the jaws to increase their width, works well. Alternatively if you've not assembled the shed you could work on the shed base.

4 Fit all the door planks together by pushing the tongues into the grooves. Squeeze them together as tightly as possible – sash clamps are ideal for this. Make sure the ends line up by resting a straight edge along them. Use a wooden or rubber mallet to move the ends into place.

TIP *Give the planks identification marks so that when they're taken apart it's possible to reassemble them in the same order.*

5 Cut three ledges of 75 x 25mm PSE timber. Cut them 20mm shorter than the overall width of the door – ours were therefore 653mm (25¾in) long. This is to allow 10mm on either side of the door that can, if necessary, be planed off to fit the door into the lining.

Lay the three ledges into place on the back of the door (the side without the 'V' grooves), two with their centres 185mm (7¼in) from the bottom and top of the door and one in the centre. Mark these locations onto the planks so that the ledges can be replaced accurately.

Rest one ledge into place and mark on it the joins between each of the door planks. Mark the screw holes so that there are two screws per plank, about 18mm in from the edge of the ledge and 18mm either side of the plank joins. Use a short length of TGV as a guide to achieve the 18mm inset for the screws.

6 Clamp all three ledges together and drill the 5mm clearance holes for the screws. A 5mm drill bit should be long enough to go through two of the ledges and make a guide mark in the third.

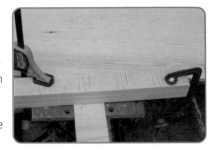

7 Countersink the holes to allow the screws to penetrate further into the planks.

When you fix the ledges, use a try square to check that they're square to the planks, measure from the top or bottom of the door to check the location of both ends of the ledge, and ensure that the ledges are 10mm in from the edges of the door. Make pencil marks to allow the ledges to be relocated.

8 Check that the door is flat on the work area and hasn't bowed. Then apply glue to the non-countersunk face of the ledges, rest them into place and

clamp both ends, ensuring that the ledges are aligned with the lines on the planks. If you have two sash clamps use them to hold the planks tight together.

Screw the ledges to the door planks using 1¼in x 8g screws. Set the drill/driver torque to a level low enough to stop the screw being driven too far into the wood. Otherwise the screws will go right through the planks and show on the front of the door.

If you don't have sash clamps, screw and glue all three ledges to one plank. Pull the next plank tight against the first and screw and glue that into place. Keep doing this until all the planks have been fixed. Chapter 1 shows an alternative method of holding planks together (page 24).

Check that each plank is pulled firmly against the ledges – if it isn't, drive the screws in a little more to pull the plank into place.

9 Wipe off excess glue using a damp cloth. Then allow the glue to dry and set the door to one side to await installation.

Making the frames

The side frames

These measure 2035mm (80in) long x 1725 (68in) from the floor to the top of wall plate. The height is a matter of choice. Our shed's sides are 1650mm (65in) high from the top of the sole plate to the underside of the wall plate (or 1725mm from floor to wall plate top). If you reduce the height the door may not fit in; if you increase it the overall height may not comply with planning requirements.

The frames are constructed of 50 x 25mm (2 x 1in) treated roofing battens, screwed together. The one with a window is built the same way as the one without a window. When deciding on the window size, take into consideration the way you'll use the shed and what needs to be placed under or alongside the window.

There's an inside and an outside to the side fames (the inside is the side with the wall plate on it), so check carefully that the window opening is in the correct location in the frame before you cut it.

Use the shed base as a template and as a flat area to work on while constructing the side frames.

1 Cut the 50 x 25mm sole plate to 2035mm long. Rest it onto the plywood base and check that it's exactly the same length.

2 Cut six 50 x 25mm uprights (studs) 1880mm (74in) long. This isn't the height of the frame: the extra length is to provide a fixing for the roof 'A' frames – they'll be cut off later.

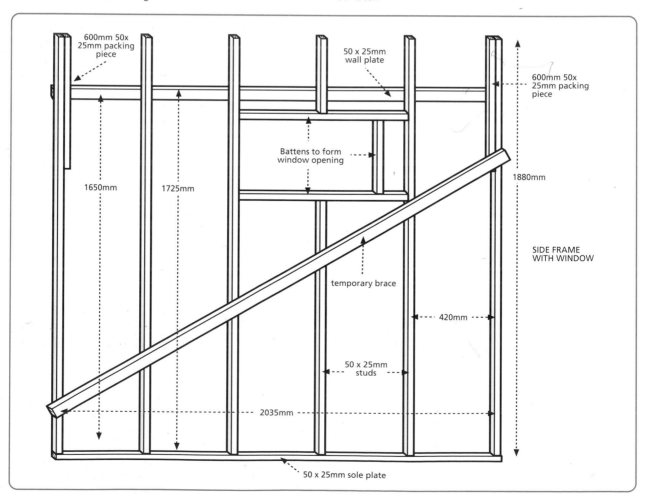

600mm 50x 25mm packing piece

50 x 25mm wall plate

600mm 50x 25mm packing piece

Battens to form window opening

1650mm

1725mm

1880mm

SIDE FRAME WITH WINDOW

temporary brace

420mm

50 x 25mm studs

2035mm

50 x 25mm sole plate

3 Lay the sole plate on the base and mark the location of the studs – one at each end and the others at 402mm (16in) centres (that is, the centres of the studs are 402mm apart).

4 Drill 5mm holes through the 50mm (2in) face of the sole plate at the centre mark for each stud.

5 Lay the sole plate onto the base on its 25mm edge. Rest the studs in position and screw each stud into place using 63mm screws. If you have difficulty holding the studs in place use a corner clamp.

Mark a line 1650mm up from the top of the sole plate on each stud. This marks the bottom of the wall plate.

6 Cut the 50 x 25mm wall plate to a length of 2035mm. Then lay one 25mm side on top of the sole plate and mark the location of the studs on the wall plate.

7 Lay the wall plate with one 50mm side resting on the studs and its bottom touching the 1650mm line. Align each stud with the stud marks on the wall plate. Drill holes between these two points and, using 63mm screws, screw through the wall plate into the studs.

8 Cut two 600mm lengths of 50 x 25mm batten and screw them into place on the inside (50mm face) and at the top of both end studs, to act as packing pieces for the 'A' frames (see plan of side pieces). 63mm deck screws will go through one piece of timber and into the next without drilling a hole. However, it's usually easier to drill 5mm clearance holes for the screws.

The side frame without a window is now completed. It will be a little floppy, so brace it temporarily with a length of batten. Mark the location of the studs onto the base and stand the side frame up out of the way.

9 Construct a second side frame the same way.

10 Taking the second frame, mark where any studs need to be cut to form the top and bottom of the window opening. For our shed window only one stud needed to be cut. When doing this allow space for the two battens that form the opening (25mm + 25mm = 50mm), and for the window lining (20mm + 20mm = 40mm). Add the total of 90mm to the window opening size.

11 Cut the stud to accommodate the window.

12 Cut two lengths of batten to fit horizontally between the remaining studs. Screw these into place, through the studs and into the top and bottom cut ends of the stud using 63mm deck screws. Check that the window opening is square using a try square.

13 The second side frame is now complete. The sides of the window opening and the continuation stud will be cut and added later (see pages 138).

14 As with the first frame, this one will also be a little floppy so brace it for now with a length of batten. Stand it up out of the way ready for use later.

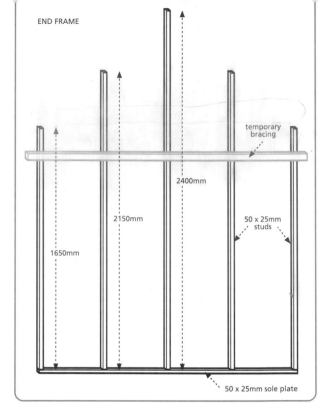

END FRAME

temporary bracing

2400mm

2150mm

1650mm

50 x 25mm studs

50 x 25mm sole plate

The end frames

The end frames measure 1780mm (70in) wide and 2400 (95.4in) high and are built using the same construction methods as the sides. Make both end frames the same way, but leave out the middle stud of one and adjust the position of the two inner studs that form the door opening. If you've made the door already it can be used as a template for the opening.

1 Cut the materials to make both end frames. You require two 50 x 25mm sole plates, 1780mm long – this is 100mm (4in) shorter than the width of the shed in order to allow for the side frames; four 50 x 25mm end studs 1650mm long, which will fit under the wall plate of the side frames so that the side and end frames interlock; four 50 x 25mm inner studs 2150mm long which will be cut to length later when the 'A' frames are in place; and one centre stud 2400mm long for the end frame without the door.

Align the end studs and the sole plate with the plywood base to ensure the frame is square. Then mark the centre of the sole plates for both end frames. This marks the location of the centre stud or the centre of the door opening.

2 For the frame without a door, mark the location of the two inner studs, half-way between the end studs and the centre stud. Drill the 5mm holes for the fixing screws in the 50mm face of the sole plate at the centre marks for each stud and screw the studs into place.

3 Drill 5mm holes in the end of the sole plate, 12.5mm in from each end, and screw the 1650mm end studs into place.

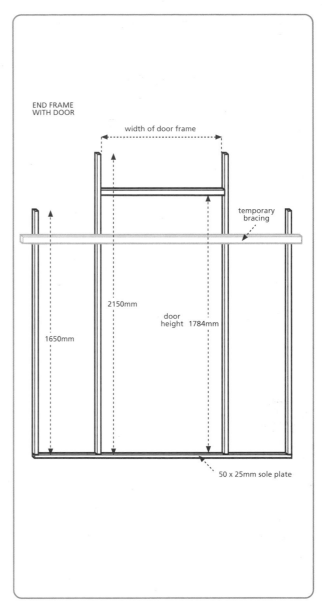

END FRAME WITH DOOR

width of door frame

temporary bracing

2150mm

door height 1784mm

1650mm

50 x 25mm sole plate

4 For the frame with a door, screw the 1650mm end studs into place as in Step 3. From the centre mark on the sole plate establish the locations of the two 2150mm-long inner studs that form the door opening. This needs to be the width of the door plus the thickness of the two door lining uprights: for our shed that means 20mm + 20mm + 673 = 713mm apart = 357mm each side of the centre mark.

Drill 5mm holes for the fixing screws in the 50mm face of the sole plate at the centre marks for each stud, and screw the studs into place using 63mm deck screws.

Cut a length of 50 x 25mm batten to fit between the two inner studs to form the head of the door. Screw this into place at the height of the door + 20mm for the door lining above the bottom of the sole plate.

5 As each end frame is completed, screw a length of batten along the top of the frame as temporary bracing. Add diagonal bracing if it's needed and stand the frame out of the way.

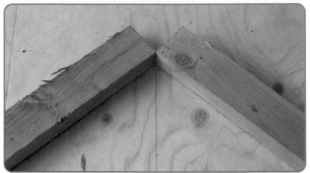

5mm screw holes

plywood
gusset plate

100 x 50mm
ridge purlin

75 x 50mm rafters
length: 1320mm

collar 50 x 25mm

35° pitch angle

The 'A' frames

Our shed is designed with a roof pitch angle of 35°. The rafters are cut from 75 x 50mm (3 x 2in) treated timber. These are held together at the apex with a gusset plate made from offcuts of the plywood used for the base. A length of 50 x 25mm batten acts as a collar and fits under a 100 x 50mm (4 x 2in) ridge purlin.

Use the base of the shed to work on. As it is the correct width, the 'A' frame rafters can be marked onto the plywood floor as a guide for each of the six frames.

1 Mark the centres of the two 1880mm (74in) ends of the base. Join these marks to give a centre line to work to.

Mark this centre line 645mm (25½in) up from one end

of the base. This mark represents the inside of the frame apex. Draw lines from the two corners of the base to this mark. This gives a full size representation of the underside of the 'A' frame. Using a length of 75 x 50mm timber as a guide, draw lines 75mm from the first ones to mark the other side (the top) of the frame.

2 Cut one of the 3.6m lengths of 75 x 50mm into two 1.8m lengths to form two rafters. Lay these along the rafter line on the base so that they meet at the 645mm mark on the centre line and touch the corners of the shed base. They will protrude beyond the base.

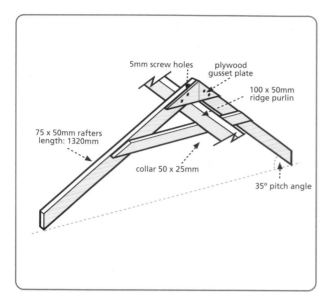

3 If you're using a chop saw set it to 35°. If you're not using a chop saw or are working to a different angle, lay a 1.8m length of 75 x 50mm rafter timber on its 75mm face between the two rafter lines so that it overlaps the centre line by about 125mm (5in).

4 Mark the position of the central line on both 50mm edges of the rafter.

SHEET 1

940mm

1220mm

lines marked to
show top and
bottom of
rafters

35° pitch
angle

front

1880mm

635mm

centre
line

SHEET 2

940mm

660mm

5 Join these marks on the 75mm faces to give the angle of the cut. Use a try square to mark the lines on the 50mm faces of the rafter. Set the sliding bevel to the angle line on the 75mm face. Mark the angle set on the sliding bevel onto a piece of plywood and write on it what it is (eg '35° angle for rafters'). In this way if the sliding bevel is subsequently readjusted the 35° angle can be re-established.

6 Cut the angle on one end of each of the two rafters and rest them on the rafter lines to check they fit. If necessary recut the angles to get a good fit. When making any adjustments for a better fit don't cut the full amount off one rafter – cut an equal amount off each.

TIP *The fit doesn't need to be perfect – the gusset plate will hold the rafters together.*

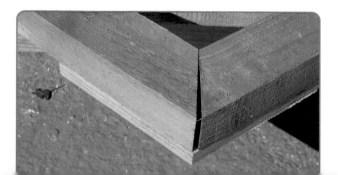

7 The rafters for our shed are 1320mm (52in) long – this allows the roof to overlap the sides by 190mm (7½in). Mark a line 1320mm from the cut end of one rafter and cut the same angle on the other end. Make sure the cut is in the right direction – both ends of the rafters should be parallel!

8 Lay the rafters along the lines so that they meet at the centre and touch the corners of the base. They should overlap the base by about 190mm. Cut a 190mm gauge of 50 x 25mm batten to check this measurement at each rafter foot (this will be used to assemble the shed). Cut the end (foot) of the other rafter to match.

9 Write 'template' on one of the rafters and use only this one as a guide for cutting the others. Use it to mark another length of 75 x 50mm and cut this at both ends. Then set the template to one side – take care not to use it yet.

The gusset plate

1 Lay the two cut rafters on the rafter lines of the base. Make sure the angles at the top of the rafters fit tightly together and that each rafter is lined up with the corners of the shed base. In order that they can't move while you're making the template for the gusset plate clamp or screw the rafters to the base.

2 Cut a 150mm (6in) section of 100 x 50mm (4 x 2in) ridge purlin timber as a guide. Stand this on end between the rafters at their apex.

3 Hold the ridge purlin section in place and use a try square, aligned with one end of the rafter, to mark the location of the gusset plate on the rafter. Do this on both rafters, then remove the ridge purlin section and mark these lines. They indicate the base of the gusset plate.

4 Cut an offcut of the base plywood 110mm (4½in) wide and at least 330mm (13in) long. Lay this on top of the apex so that it just touches the marks you've made for the base of the gusset plate. Then mark along the rafters onto the underside of the plywood to show the angle of the apex.

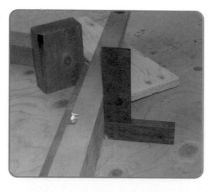

5 Join these lines up and cut along the lines to form the gusset plate.

6 Rest the gusset plate on top of the rafters and check that the bottom edge just touches the line and the top edges are flush with the tops of the rafters (they must not protrude above the rafters or they'll interfere with the roof). When it's a good fit write 'template' on it and cut the other five gusset plates to match.

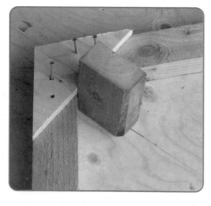

7 Unclamp or unscrew the rafters. Drill 5mm holes in the gusset plate and screw and glue it to one of the rafters. Check that the rafters are still aligned with the rafter lines and screw and glue the other rafter into place.

Reposition the 100 x 50mm ridge purlin section and check that it touches the gusset and the rafters.

8 Cut a 790mm (31in) length of 50 x 25mm batten to form a collar. Rest this under the 100 x 50mm ridge purlin section. Mark the angle of the rafters on both ends of the batten and cut to these lines. Screw the collar into place, making sure that both ends are flush with the top of the rafter. Make a gauge to check that the collar is parallel to the gusset plate. Don't glue the collars into place.

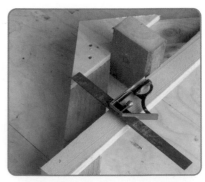

The 'A' frame should now be quite rigid when you pick it up.

9 Make up the other five 'A' frames the same way. Treat all cut ends of timber with a suitable treatment, then stand them to one side ready for use.

Cladding using feather-edge

Cladding the side frames

You can choose any type of cladding you want for your shed, but remember, it's the cladding that gives the shed its strength, and some types (*eg* vertical cladding and corrugated iron) won't provide enough. To overcome this some form of 'racking' will be required in such cases, to keep the side structure in shape. 9mm plywood would be ideal for this. It could be fixed either to the inside of the frame or to the outside with the cladding added on top of it.

The cladding can be fixed to both side frames before assembling the shed. This adds rigidity to the frames when handling them but also makes them heavy. The end frames are clad after the shed has been assembled.

Our shed was clad with ex 125 x 25mm feather-edge boards spaced so that there's an exposed area of 100mm (4in). Cladding the shed using shiplap board after the frames have been assembled is covered later in the chapter. Buy the longest lengths of feather-edge you can: that way there'll be less wastage when it's cut to length.

1 To ensure that the side frame is square while it's being clad, lay one side frame flat on the shed base and screw or clamp it so that the edges of the frame are aligned with the base edges. Remember to remove the fixing screws before the cladding is applied over them!

2 Lay a length of feather-edge on the frame and align one end with the end of the frame. Mark the other end and cut along this line. A chop saw set to 0° is ideal for this.

Alternatively, instead of cutting one length of cladding at a time fix all the planks so that they align exactly at one end and then saw off all the ends simultaneously. If you're sawing by hand take care not to damage the thin edge of the cladding.

Note that it's better not to saw off the treated ends of feather-edge – they'll have been pressure treated so that the treatment penetrates a long way into the end grain. To avoid removing one cut end, align the treated ends and cut off the others.

3 With its thick edge to the bottom of the frame, fix the lowermost section of cladding to the sole plate using 38mm oval galvanised nails.

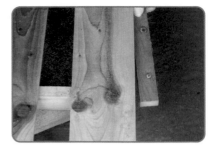

Allow the bottom board to overlap the sole plate so that it will cover the edge of the plywood base and a little more when the frame is stood in place. For our shed this overlap was 50mm – use the 50mm face of a piece of 50 x 25mm batten as a depth guide. The oval nails can be driven below the surface of the feather-edge using a nail punch and a hammer.

If you prefer you can use 1in x 6g screws to fix the feather-edge. This method of fixing vibrates the frame less than hammering in nails, which is important if you're cladding a frame after the framework has been assembled.

Use a length of batten, on its 50mm face, as a guide to the location of the nails going into the sole plate.

4 To space the remaining feather-edge uniformly, use a 100mm gauge made from an offcut of batten. Write '100mm gauge' on it. Alternatively, set a combination square to the correct setting. The gauge is to measure the amount of timber that's exposed, not the amount overlapped. This will be referred to as the 'exposure'. Using the gauge will ensure that each board overlaps the one below it by about 25mm and covers any nails or screws in its upper edge.

5 Lay the next feather-edge board in place overlapping the one fixed in Step 3, with the thick edge at the bottom. Hold the 100mm gauge to get the correct overlap and nail it into place. Fix the top (thin) edge of the feather-edge to every stud using 30mm galvanised clout nails, 25mm or less from the top edge so that they're hidden by the overlap of the next plank. Use 38mm galvanised oval nails to fix the bottom edge. These go through the top of the feather-edge below and into a stud, and can be punched below the surface so they're out of sight.

When hammering nails into timber, blunt the sharp end of the nail by hitting it with a hammer. This may help to stop the wood splitting. Drilling a small (2mm) hole for the nail will also help.

If you need to join the feather-edge because one length was cut too short, screw a piece of 25 x 50mm batten to one side of the stud and fix the cladding to that.

6 When you've aligned, cut and fixed three or four more boards, using the 100mm gauge to space them, check the measurements. Measure the distance at both ends of the frame, from the bottom of the last plank fixed to the top of the wall plate. This should be the same at both ends. If it isn't, make small adjustments on the next few boards to get them right. Don't adjust by more than a few mm at a time – it will be noticed. Continue to fix the cladding.

7 When there are only four or five more boards needed to reach the top, measure the distance left to cover and adjust the spacing of the cladding to achieve a uniform overlap.

8 Clad the frame to within two boards of the top – it will need to be cut around the rafters later. Treat all cut ends of timber and allow it to dry, then lift frame out of the way. You'll need two people to do this.

9 Clad the other side frame, using the same method as described above but cutting the cladding around the window opening.

Cladding round the window opening

1 If you've not already done so, cut a length of 50 x 25mm batten to form one vertical side of the window opening and a short length to continue the cut stud above the window. Screw these into place.

2 Cut the feather-edge at the sides of the window opening to length and fix it into place in the same way as the other boards.

3 The boards along the top and bottom of the window opening may also need to be cut to fit. If so mark them carefully using a combination square.

3 Use a jigsaw to cut off the excess. Then treat all cut ends of timber and allow to dry.

4 The 75 x 25mm PSE window frame can either be fitted now, or after the shed has been assembled. To install it, cut lengths of 75 x 25mm PSE to fit along the bottom and top of the window opening. Push these into place so that they're flush with the feather-edge cladding and fix them to the 50 x 25mm lengths that form the top and bottom of the opening using 1½in x 8g screws. If the screws are located carefully they'll be hidden by the window glass and beading.
    Cut two shorter lengths for the side pieces and fit these into place in the same way.

Assembling the side and end frames

Two people are needed to handle the sections – more if possible. As the assembly proceeds, prop each frame so that it can't fall over. Do not work in a high wind!

1 Set the shed base into place on a firm level footing as recommended at the beginning of this chapter. Ensure that the floor joists are well supported and level in both directions.

3 Having supported the frame in position, screw through the sole plate of the side frame into each of the joists using 63mm deck screws or 2½in x 8g screws. It may be necessary to drill holes at a slight angle so that the screws are driven into the floor joists.

4 Stand the other side frame in place, prop it securely and screw it to the base.

Rest the other side frame into place (once again taking care not to damage the overlapping cladding if the frame is being assembled in its clad form). Fit the end stud of the end frame under the wall plate of the side frame. Prop the frame securely.

2 Stand one clad side frame in place on the base. Screw or clamp temporary lengths of batten to the frame to support it. Make sure the frame lines up with both ends of the base – use a rubber mallet or hammer and a block of wood to move the frame into place. Take care not to damage the bottom row of cladding where it overlaps the base.

From here on the shed is shown being assembled with both clad and unclad frames in order to demonstrate both ways of putting it together.

5 Stand the back end frame in place and clamp it to the side frames. The 50 x 25mm end studs fit under the wall plate of the side frames. While one person holds the end frame, screw it to the side frames using four 2in x 8g screws, and to the base using 63mm deck screws.

TIP *You may need to loosen the screws that secure the side frame to the base to allow the end frame to fit under its wall plate. Once the end frame is fitted tighten the screws again.*

6 Once the back end frame is fixed to the base and the side frames, rest the end frame with the door opening on the base and fix it to the side frames and the base in the same way. Use at least two screws on either side of the door opening. There's no need to angle these – they'll go directly into the floor joist.

Check that all the corners are upright. If they're not, push and prop them until they are. Screw any unfixed corners together and check that they're still upright. Use at least four 2in x 8g screws for each corner.

The framework should now be rigid and is ready for the 'A' frames to be fitted.

Fitting the 'A' frames and ridge purlin

Make sure the end and side frames are square, upright and fixed securely together before you start.

Safety Fitting the 'A' frames is a job that requires at least two people. Also, take great care when using stepladders.

1 Lift the first 'A' frame into place at one end of the shed. It can rest upside down on the wall plates and be rotated into position.

2 Stand the 'A' frame upright and rest it against the studs of the end frame and against the packing pieces fixed when the side frames were built (Step 8 on page 131). The gusset plate must face the inside of the shed. Ensure that the ends (feet) of the rafters overlap the wall plates by the same amount each side – use the 190mm gauge you cut for the 'A' frame assembly to check this.

Clamp and then screw the 'A' frame to the studs of the end frame using 63mm deck screws. Then drill 5mm holes in the side frame studs and the packing pieces and screw through these into the 'A' frame, using 3in x 8g screws.

The 'A' frame should be quite secure at this stage.

5 Drill a 5mm hole in the 25mm edge of each collar and screw up through these into the ridge purlin, using 3in x 8g screws.

3 Lift an 'A' frame into place at the other end, with the gusset plate towards the inside. Clamp it to the studs and screw it into place. Use the 190mm gauge you cut when making the 'A' frames (Step 8, page 135) to check that the feet of the rafters overlap by the same amount each side.

4 Ease the 100 x 50mm (4 x 2in) ridge purlin into place by sliding it between the collar and the gusset plate of the front 'A' frame and back between the collar and the gusset plate of the back 'A' frame, so that it rests against the central stud of the latter. It will need to be kept horizontal as it's passed though the

space between the collar and the gusset plate of the frames.

Measure the distances between the 'A' frames at foot and apex – these should be the same. If they're not, adjust the frames until the measurements are equal. Check that they're still vertical.

6 Remove one screw from the collars of each of the remaining four 'A' frames and twist the collar down out of the way, so that the 'A' frame can be slid into place over the ridge purlin. It doesn't matter which side of the studs the 'A' frames are placed or which way the gussets face.

7 Use the 190mm gauge at both feet of each 'A' frame to check that it's aligned. Then clamp the frame into place and screw into it through the side frame studs. Screw the

collar back into place. Repeat this procedure for each 'A' frame.

Check the frames are upright by measuring between their feet and between their apexes, then screw up through their collars into the ridge purlin. If necessary cut the ridge purlin so that it is 50mm (2in) in front of the front end 'A' frames and lines up with the studs at the front.

8 Saw the protruding ends of the studs level with the 'A' frames. Treat all cut ends of timber.

Final feather-edge side cladding

If the side frames were not clad when fitted you need to clad them now, following the instructions set out on pages 144. If they were clad, two more lengths of cladding will need to be added under and around the feet of the rafters.

1 Fit short lengths of 50 x 25mm batten alongside the rafter 'A' frames for the cladding to be fixed to.

2 Screw them to the rafters or the wall plate or both. There's no need to angle the top if it's awkward to do so.

3 Use the 100mm gauge and a short length of feather-edge as a depth gauge to indicate how much timber needs to be removed from the feather-edge to allow the board to fit around the rafter.

4 Cut a length of feather-edge to fit along the full length of the shed. Hold it in place and mark the location of both sides of each of the rafters.

5 Use a try square to extend these rafter location lines and use the depth gauge to mark the depth of the notches to be removed from the feather-edge to allow it to fit around the joists.

6 Use a jigsaw or universal saw to cut along the two rafter location lines. To cut the line along the back of the cut-out made using the depth gauge, either chop the timber out with a chisel or use a jigsaw.

Fix the feather-edge into place, using the 100mm gauge to check the exposure is correct.

7 Cut short lengths of feather-edge to fit between the rafters. Fix them into place, using the 100mm gauge to get the correct exposure. It may be necessary to cut the tops off these pieces so that they align with the top of the rafters.

8 Complete the cladding on the other side in the same way.

Cladding the end frames

The end frames are clad when the frames have been fixed together, the 'A' frames installed, and the side frame cladding completed.

9 Screw a length of 50 x 25mm batten vertically to each corner to conceal the ends of the feather-edge board on the side frames. The top of this batten will need to be cut to the angle of the roof, and the bottom flush with the bottom of the lowermost feather-edge board.

10 To support the cladding at the apex and along the gable end, cut two lengths of 50 x 25mm batten to fit between the inner studs of the end frame and the apex, and two to fit between the inner studs of the

end frame and the corner pieces just fitted. It's not essential to cut the ends at an angle but it makes a neater job. Use 63mm deck screws to fix these battens flush with the top of both the end 'A' frames.

11 Clad the end frames in the same way as the side frames. Cut lengths of feather-edge about 100mm longer than required and hold them in place. Mark the correct length and cut to this line.

Use the 100mm template to get the exposure of the feather-edge accurate. Cut the cladding so that it butts up to the 50 x 25mm corner pieces fitted earlier and fits around the door opening (the door frame will be fitted later). If you need to cut the cladding to fit over the top of the opening you may find it easier to fit it into place and then cut off the excess using a jigsaw.

It's important to align the cladding on the end frames with the cladding on the sides – despite the 50 x 25mm corner piece separating them, any differences in level will be noticeable if you don't.

12 Screw or nail the cladding into place until the gable end is reached.

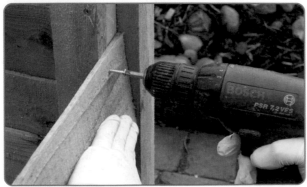

TIP *When cladding the gable ends, cut each piece of cladding longer than required. Using the 100mm gauge to locate it properly, clamp it in place and mark the angle to be sawn off. Remove the cladding and saw to this line.*

13 When the apex has been clad check that the front sole plate is fixed to the base on either side of the doorway and saw off the sole plate where it crosses the opening.

Fitting the door lining

The door lining is made from 75 x 25mm (3 x 1in) PSE and is fixed after the cladding is complete.

1 Cut one length of 75 x 25mm PSE to form the top (head) of the lining. For our shed this was the width of the door plus the thickness of the two door lining uprights (673mm + 20mm + 20mm = 713mm).

2 Locate the head of the doorframe in place, making sure it lines up with the cladding. Drill and countersink two 5mm holes in the timber and screw it into place. Make sure that the 2in x 8g screws go into the 50 x 25mm inner studs.

3 Cut the two 75 x 25mm PSE uprights so that they're a tight fit between the head and the floor. These are the height of the door (1785mm). Align the uprights with the cladding and screw them to the frame opening using 2in x 8g screws.

4 A drip moulding can be made using a length of 21mm Scotia glued or nailed into place. This can be fitted before or after the door is hung.

5 When both the end frames have been clad, apply good quality timber treatment to the whole shed, taking care to soak the ends of the timbers.

Fixing shiplap: an alternative cladding system

As with the feather-edge, the side frames can be clad before they're assembled. However, the pictures in this section show the frames being clad after assembly.

Note that the instructions for feather-edge cladding given above contain additional information pertinent to this procedure.

1 Before starting to apply the cladding, check that the frames are aligned with, and fixed to, the base and that the corners are screwed together and vertical.

2 Fit four vertical corner pieces of 50 x 25mm PSE. Clamp each length into place with one end just below the level of the plywood base. Mark and cut the other end at an angle so that it's flush with the 'A' frame.

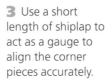

3 Use a short length of shiplap to act as a gauge to align the corner pieces accurately.

To prevent the fixings being seen from the outside, screw the corner pieces into place from the inside of the shed, using 1½in x 8g screws.

4 Cut lengths of shiplap to fit along the full length of each side and along the back. Use these pieces as templates to cut the other lengths for the sides and back.

5 Fix the bottom shiplap planks on both sides and the back. Clamp each of them into place and check that they hide the edges of the plywood base and that are aligned with the planks round both corners.

A combination square can be used to locate the lowermost lengths of shiplap (the side and end pieces) the same distance above the floor.

Each board can be either nailed from the front using 38mm galvanised oval nails or screwed from the back using 2¼in or 2½in x 8g screws through the studs or the sole plate. The ends of the shiplap cannot be screwed from the back – nail these instead.

6 Fit shiplap planks up one side of the shed. If you use nails, having a second person hold a heavy item such as a club hammer against the inside of the frame will stop it from bouncing while the nails are driven in. Drive the heads of the nails below the surface using a nail punch and hammer.

If you use screws driven in from the inside, note that the 50 x 25mm roofing battens used for the frame won't be a uniform size so you may need to countersink some of the holes to allow 2¼in x 8g screws to bite into the shiplap. Alternatively, 2½in x 8g screws could be used. Place the screws so that they're driven into the thick section of the shiplap – they will show if they penetrate the face of the thin section.

After fitting every three or four planks, check to make sure that the shiplap is the same distance down from the wall plate at each end. If it isn't, the next row can be adjusted by either lifting the shiplap a little or planing a few millimetres off the tongue. Never adjust a plank more than 2–3mm – it will show.

Fitting the window lining

When the cladding reaches near the top of the window opening, fit the 100 x 25mm (4 x 1in) PSE window sill and the 75 x 25mm PSE head and uprights.

1 Cut a length of 100 x 25mm PSE about 150mm longer than the window opening is wide. Hold this against the opening with the same amount overlapping at each side and mark the width of the opening onto one 25mm face of the timber.

2 Decide on the amount of sill to protrude in front of the shiplap. Mark the amount of timber that needs to be cut out (55mm) to enable the sill to fit into the window opening while leaving the required amount of sill protruding. Draw a line to this depth (55mm) on both the marks made in Step 1. Set a combination square to this depth and mark a line on both ends to demarcate the area to be cut out.

3 Saw along these lines to remove the corners of the window sill.

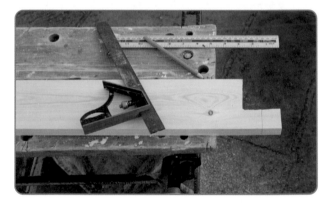

4 The horns created by cutting out the corners will be a little longer than required. Rest the sill in place and decide on the required length of the horns. Mark this length on each horn, remove the sill and saw to these lines.

5 Round off the corners of the horns and smooth off the sill using a belt sander. Then screw the sill into place using 1½in x 8g screws. Make sure that the screws go into the 50 x 25mm batten and not the shiplap. The sill can be screwed into place from underneath, through the lower horizontal batten.

6 Cut a length of 75 x 25mm PSE to fit into the top of the window opening. Align it flush with the outside face of the shiplap and screw it into place. Then cut the two 75 x 25mm PSE uprights for the sides of the window opening and screw these into place, aligning them with the shiplap.

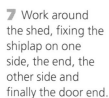

7 Work around the shed, fixing the shiplap on one side, the end, the other side and finally the door end. Cut the boards around the feet of the rafters, around the door, and along the bottom and top of the window

opening. Take care that the shiplap boards on all four sides are aligned.

8 Cut and fix the shiplap at the gable ends. For more details see the section on feather-edge cladding.

9 When the cladding is complete, apply good quality timber treatment to the whole shed, taking care to soak the ends of the timbers.

The roof

At this stage it is necessary to decide whether the shed needs a fascia or not. The fascia is a length of timber that can be used to carry the guttering, so if the shed is to have guttering one should be fitted. Details about fitting a fascia can be found in the section dealing with cedar shingle roofing (page 151).

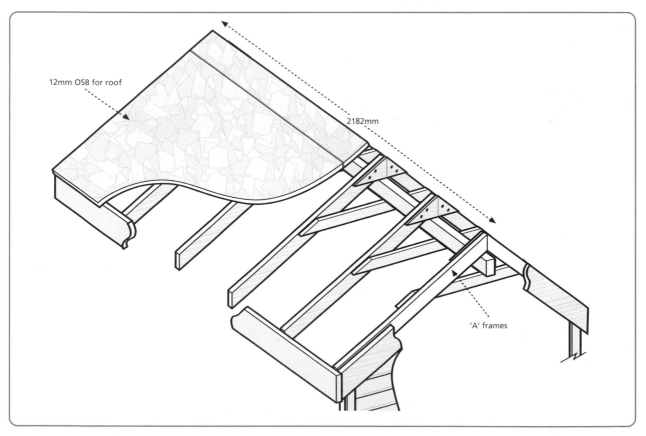

12mm OSB for roof

2182mm

'A' frames

Fixing OSB roof decking

The roof decking is made from 12mm Oriented Strand Board (OSB). Our shed was built without a fascia, but if you decide to fit one then the narrow strips of plywood cut to fill in the top of the roof will have to be wider, because the roof will need to overlap the feet of the rafters more.

If you intend to fix guttering a fascia will make the job a lot easier.

Safety A small amount of tower scaffold may make this job easier and safer. In addition note that this is at least a two-person job, while more people than that would make it even easier.

1 Fix a length of 50 x 25mm batten (with its 25mm edge against the feather-edge or cladding) onto each slope of the gable ends. This apex batten is to allow the roof to overlap at the front and back of the shed; to give the OSB roof decking something to fix to; to provide something for the roofing felt to wrap around; and to provide a fixing for the bargeboard. These battens need to protrude 12mm beyond the feet of the rafters.

Cut an angle at one end of each batten so that they meet at the apex of the roof, and square at the other end to meet the batten that's fixed along the bottom edge of the roof decking. Drill four holes in the 25mm side of each and, using 4in x 8g screws, screw it into place level with the top of the 'A' frames.

If a fascia is being fitted, allow the batten to protrude 35mm – this will allow for the thickness of the fascia. For more details on fitting a fascia, see the section on page 151 on fitting bargeboards and fascia on a cedar shingle roof.

2 To cut the OSB, first measure the width of the roof from apex batten to apex batten. This is the length the OSB decking needs to be. For our shed this was 2182mm, but measure your own shed to get the correct measurement. Cut two 2440 x 1220mm sheets of OSB to this length.

3 Using 1in x 8g screws, screw through the OSB, fix a length of 35 x 18mm batten along one 2182mm edge of each of the two large sheets. This is for the felt to wrap around (50 x 25mm batten can be used, but if it is the narrow section of OSB at the top of the roof will be wider).

4 Rest one large sheet into place, clamp it and screw it to the rafters using 1½in x 8g screws 20mm in from the edge of the OSB and at 150mm intervals down the line of the rafters. Do the same with the large sheet on the other side.

TIP *Clamping the OSB sheets into place to start with allows them to be aligned easily.*

5 Measure the width of OSB required to fill the top section of the roof. One piece needs to stop at the apex of the 'A' frames. The other needs to be 12mm longer to overlap the piece just fitted. Mark these strips on the OSB and cut them out using a circular saw or a universal hard point saw. Then rest the strips in place and screw them to the rafters.

6 If necessary plane off excess OSB along the ridge, using a hand or power plane. Check all the screws are below the surface of the sheet before you start.

Felting the roof

Always follow the manufacturer's instructions for whatever felt and adhesive you use. Our shed was roofed using Marley Shed Felt. Where it overlapped another section of felt it was stuck down with Aqua Seal Felt Adhesive. The felt was nailed every 50mm at the overlaps, with the nails at least 20mm in from edge of the felt.

Safety Only use a retractable knife and ensure that the blade is always retracted when not in use.

1 Cut one length of felt about 150mm (6in) longer than the roof to allow it to wrap around the battens. Hold it in place on the roof and fix it with clamps, using offcuts of wood to protect the felt.

The sequence when applying the felt is: fix the bottom sheets first; overlap the next sheets onto these; and fit the ridge sheet last so that it overlaps both sides.

2 Make chalk marks 50mm down from the top of the felt to locate the nails. Using 13mm galvanised clout nails, nail along the top of the felt to hold it in place while the bottom and sides are nailed. Nailing on top of rafters is easiest, since there's less bounce from the OSB sheet.

> **TIP** *Short nails are easier to hammer in if they're held with long nose pliers.*

3 Wrap the felt around the batten at the bottom edge (eaves) of the roof and nail it into place at 50mm intervals, using 13mm galvanised clout nails. It's a good idea to make a 50mm gauge to determine the spacing for the nails.

4 Fold the felt carefully at the corners and use a 30mm galvanised clout nail to fix it under the front edge. On a cold day use a hairdryer to warm the felt so that it folds easily, first taking all necessary precautions to ensure the safe use of electricity – that is, do not work on a wet day; plug the extension lead into an RCD (safety plug); and run the extension in such a way that it can't get damaged and won't be tripped over. See Chapter 1 for more details of electrical safety.

5 Bend the edges of felt around the battens on each gable and nail them into place using 13mm galvanised nails at 50mm intervals.

6 Fix the felt the same way on the other side of the roof.

7 Cut a second length of felt for the first side. Make a chalk line 75mm down from the top of the felt already fitted to mark the required overlap. (The amount of overlap is up to you, provided you comply with the manufacturer's minimum requirements.) Apply adhesive to the felt above the chalk line.

8 Place the second length of felt so that it meets the chalk line and force it down onto the adhesive. Nail it along the top to hold it in place as in Step 2. Then nail it along the join using 13mm clout nails, spaced at 50mm intervals.

Wrap it under the front and back gable end battens and nail it on the underside of the battens at 50mm intervals.

Repeat Steps 7 and 8 on the other side of the roof.

9 Measure the width of the piece of felt required to fit over the ridge to ensure that it overlaps the other sheet by the recommended amount. Cut it to width and glue and nail it into place.

Cutting and fitting bargeboards for a felt roof

You should have decided by now whether or not a fascia is to be fitted. No fascia has been fitted to the felt-roof version of our shed, but for details about fitting a fascia see the section on fitting bargeboards and fascias to a cedar shingle roof.

The 75 x 25mm PSE bargeboards fix, at both ends of the shed, to the gable end battens that the roofing felt is wrapped around. Cut and fit each pair of bargeboards (back and front) separately. Do not assume that the front and back of the shed are exactly the same.

1 Using 50mm (2in) lost head galvanised nails, temporarily nail a length of 75 x 25mm PSE to an end batten (through the felt) so that it aligns with the top of the roof and overlaps at the eaves by at least 50mm. Leave enough nail protruding so that it can be pulled out using a claw hammer.

2 Use a spirit level to mark a vertical line on the bargeboard at the apex of the roof. This gives the angle of the cut required in Step 3. More details of how to do this can be found in the section on fitting bargeboards and fascia to a cedar shingle roof and the section on building a dog kennel in Chapter 2.

3 Cut the marked angle on one end of both lengths of 75 x 25mm PSE and hold them in place to check the angle is correct. Adjust the angle if necessary. Then, using 50mm lost head galvanised nails, nail both boards temporarily into place so that the join at the apex is a good fit.

4 Use a straight edge to align the ends of the bargeboards with the edge of the roof and make a mark at this point. The bargeboards can overlap the edge of the roof if required but there's a danger of walking into the overlap if they do! Using a spirit level as a guide, draw a vertical line from these marks down the face of each bargeboard.

5 Use a spirit level as a guide to mark a horizontal line to meet the vertical lines drawn in Step 4. Remove the bargeboards and make these cuts.

6 Treat the backs and ends of the boards.

7 When the treatment is dry, nail the boards into place using 50mm lost head galvanised nails. Punch the nails below the surface.

8 Treat the fronts of the bargeboards once they're fixed. Fix the other pair of bargeboards at the other end in the same way.

Cutting and fitting bargeboards and fascia for a cedar shingle roof

Unless you're fitting a fascia or a cedar shingle roof this section may not be of interest to you – if not, go to the section on glazing the window.

The bargeboards are made using 125 x 25mm PSE, while the fascia is made using 100 x 25mm PSE.

1 Screw 50 x 25mm battens to the apex at both gable ends of the shed so that one 50mm face is flush with the gable. These will provide a fixing for the bargeboards and hold them 25mm clear of the shiplap cladding. They need to be fixed so that they're 25mm above the 'A' frame. This is to allow the top of the roofing battens for the shingles to lay flush with the top of the bargeboards. The 3in x 8g fixing screws should go through the shiplap into the battens on the 'A' frame.

2 Clamp a length of 125 x 25mm PSE timber in place to represent one side of the bargeboard and use a spirit level as a guide to make a vertical mark at the top of the board.

Cut this angle on one end of the four bargeboards (two for each end) and clamp them into place to see how well they fit. Adjust the cuts until the bargeboards fit well and sit flush with the top of the bargeboard battens. Do not fix them yet.

3 Cut the 100 x 25mm PSE for the fascias to length so that they fit between the bargeboards at each end. These will be fixed to the feet of the rafters.

4 To align the fascias with the roof, fix a temporary length of batten (using 50mm galvanised wire nails) about 25mm up from the feet of the rafters (use an offcut of bargeboard as a gauge) and another batten 160mm further up the roof. Don't drive the nails in fully – they'll need to be removed later. Rest a straight edge on top of these battens to set the height of the fascias.

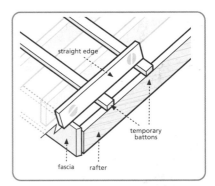

straight edge
temporary battens
fascia   rafter

5 Screw the fascias to the feet of the rafters on both sides of the shed. Use a straight edge to align them with the temporary battens on the roof.

6 Use a spirit level as a guide to mark the feet of the bargeboards (see the section on fitting bargeboards to the feather-edge shed). Allow the feet of the bargeboards to overlap the fascia by 5mm or so. Cut and fix all four bargeboards.

Hanging cedar shingles

The bargeboard and fascia must be fitted before the cedar shingles are added.

Safety Tower scaffolding may make this job easier and safer. Also note that it's a job best done with two people.

1 Do a dummy run on the ground to establish the best spacing of the battens and shingles.

2 Cut sixteen 50 x 25mm roofing battens to the correct length. They should fit between the bargeboards or the battens to which the bargeboards are fixed. The first batten is nailed 25mm away from the feet of the rafters (and the fascia). Space the remaining battens at 160mm centres and use 50mm (2in) galvanised wire nails to fix four battens to the rafters. Then measure to check that both ends of the fourth batten are the same distance from

the apex of the roof (see Step 3). Use a builders' line pulled tight between the bargeboards to check that the battens are straight. If they aren't, they can be pulled into line as they're nailed.

TIP *It's easier to measure from the top of one batten to the top of the next rather than to measure from centre to centre. However, it will speed the job up even more if you cut a 110m gauge that fits between two sets of battens.*

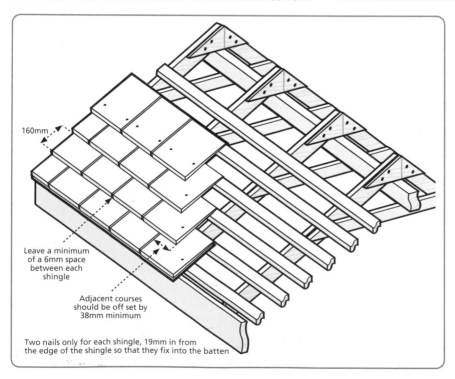

160mm

Leave a minimum of a 6mm space between each shingle

Adjacent courses should be off set by 38mm minimum

Two nails only for each shingle, 19mm in from the edge of the shingle so that they fix into the batten

3 Before the last three or four battens are fixed, check the distance to the apex of the roof to ensure that the spacing between the battens can be maintained at 160mm. Adjust the spacing of the rest if necessary.

The top batten is fixed at the apex regardless of the spacing, so that the top battens on each side will touch there.

4 Fix the battens on the other side of the roof in the same way.

5 The illustration shows the correct spacing details for the cedar shingles. Shingles are laid with the thick end downwards and nailed about two-thirds distance up the shingle to a batten.

6 Fix the first row of shingles, making sure they overlap the fascia by 75mm. This will allow rain to run off into the guttering, if any is fitted. Cut a 75mm gauge to check the overlap.

7 Check the shingles overlap the bargeboard by 50mm. Cut a 50mm gauge to check this.

8 The shingles need to be spaced 6mm apart – use a 6mm drill bit as a gauge.

Shingles are far from uniform in shape and size. If a spacing of 6mm is attempted at the bottom of the shingle, there's a good chance it will be quite different at the top. As you lay the shingles you'll get a 'feel' for how they should be spaced. But remember that there must be a distance of 38mm between the joins of different layers (see plan).

Nail the shingles to the batten using two 30mm galvanised clout nails per shingle. The nails must be at least 19mm in from the edges of the shingle. On our shed the exposure of a shingle – the distance between the bottom of a shingle and the bottom of the shingle in the row above – was set at 160mm. Cut a 160mm gauge to rest on the shingles to get this spacing accurate.

9 Work along and up the roof until the apex is reached on one side. Then start work on the other side. This will enable you to reach the apex of the roof from inside the shed, between the rafters.

10 The top two rows of shingles will need to be cut so that they don't protrude above the apex. When deciding how much to cut off, try to keep the overlap of the shingles about the same. On our shed the very top row of shingles is 180mm long and the next row down 290mm. This gives an overlap of 110mm.

> **TIP** *Even if you have a power saw, cut the shingles with a hand saw – they're quite delicate and are easily damaged by a power saw.*

11 The ridges can be fitted as the apex of the roof is completed. This allows you to work from inside the shed. The ridges are overlapped by 200mm and nailed into place using 50mm galvanised nails.

> **TIP** *The ridges are made from two sections of cedar joined together. These are overlapped in alternate directions. Try to alternate the ridges so that those with the same direction of overlap don't coincide.*

Glazing the window

Decide whether to use glass or perspex in the window. See Chapter 1 for details of how to cut glass and the regulations regarding the use of glass.

Fitting the window lining is described for the feather-edge-clad shed on page 138 and for the shiplap-clad shed on page 147.

See Chapter 6 for more information about glazing.

1 Make a template of cardboard or hardboard to fit the window opening. This will act as a guide to the person who cuts the glass.

2 Mitre the corners of an inner and an outer set (four lengths to each set) of glass bead or quadrant to form the inner and outer frame to hold the glass or perspex in place. When glazing the shiplap shed 22mm quadrant beading was used.

3 Using 30mm galvanised oval nails, nail the outer set of beading into place. To stop the wood splitting either blunt the end of each nail or drill a small (2mm) hole.

If extra waterproofing is required, add a bead of silicon glazing mastic on the outside where the glass or perspex joins the beading.

4 Rest the glass or perspex into place from the inside.

5 Using 30mm galvanised oval nails, nail the inner beading into place to secure the glass or perspex.

Fitting the door

Two people will be needed for this job.

1 Decide which way you want the door to open (on our shed it opens outwards).

2 Screw a length of 50 x 25mm batten to the front of the floor joist in the door opening, to rest the door on while it's being hung.

3 Our shed door was hung using 300mm (12in) galvanised 'T' hinges. To help align the hinges, mark the location of the centre of the door ledges on the door lining. For our shed these were 185mm from the top and bottom.

4 Hold the central screw hole of the hinge over the central line for one ledge and align the back of the hinge with the edge of the door lining. Drill a 2mm pilot hole through the centre screw hole and screw the hinge to the edge of the door lining using a 1½in x 8g screw. With the hinge aligned with the edge of the door lining, drill the other two pilot holes and drive in the screws. Fit the other hinge in the same way and flip the hinges out of the way.

TIP *Rest the door on two or three pieces of cardboard to give it a little more clearance above the floor when it's hung.*

5 With a helper standing inside the shed (with a pencil!), push the door into place resting on the supporting batten and the cardboard. If the door is found to be too large, draw a line on the inside where it touches the frame. Then remove the door and plane off the timber to this line.

Safety Fix the door into a workbench or some other form of support to hold it firmly while it's being planed.

6 Push the door back into place, resting on the cardboard, with your helper inside to support it and check that it now fits. Flip the hinges onto the door and drill 2mm pilot holes into the door through their screw holes. Screw the door into place using 1½in x 8g screws. Better still use 1½in countersunk, slot-head galvanised screws.

7 With the door held shut, use 30mm galvanised oval nails to fix two short lengths of parting bead or a similar thin timber on the inside of the door lining for the door to close onto.

8 Fit some device to keep the door closed. Our shed had a galvanised turn button, but you might want to consider fitting a more secure lock or perhaps an alarm to deter thieves.

9 Treat the shed thoroughly with a good quality timber treatment. Then enjoy your shed!

BUILDING A GREENHOUSE

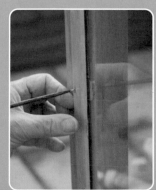

This is perhaps the most complex of the structures described in this book, partly because the measurements need to be very accurate but also because of the complex nature of the glass bars.

For this construction there'll be no machining to cut grooves or rebates but it is recommended that you have a chop saw to cut exact angles. Those of you who can machine rebates will be able to save a lot of money by not having to buy beading (strip wood). All the timbers used are stock sizes and the glass is horticultural-size or cut from horticultural-size glass.

Apart from the enjoyment of the job, the advantage of making your own wooden greenhouse is the opportunity it provides to have one to the exact size you want – it

Materials

Quantity	Materials	Purpose
4	2m lengths 100 x 50mm treated timber	Plinth
9	2.8m lengths 44 x 44mm PSE	Rafters; door frame; end frames; door
8	2m lengths 33 x 44mm PSE	Frame uprights; wall plates; door; uprights;
5	3m lengths 33 x 44mm PSE	rafters
10	36 x 8mm bead (strip wood)	Glass battens
7	8 x 8mm bead (strip wood)	Glass battens
1	3m length glass bead	Glass battens
1	1m length 21mm Scotia	Glass battens
14	2.4m lengths of 32 x 4mm 'D' shape	Glass cover strips
8	4.7m lengths of 38 x 18mm treated roofing batten	Staging
11	1m lengths 50 x 50mm treated deck spindles	Staging legs
1	2m length 100 x 25mm PSE	Ridge
8	2m lengths 75 x 25mm PSE	Sills; ridge cap; staging fronts; vent
20	3m lengths 13 x 100mm TGV (PMVJ)	Cladding and door
4	2m lengths 100mm bull-nose skirting	
50	25mm x 0.8mm galvanised nails	
50	25mm oval galvanised nails	Cladding
8	Fischer fixings	Fixing plinth to paving
12	5in x 12g screws	
20	4in x 10g screws	
20	3in x 10g screws	
	Low modulus silicon mastic	
1 box	¾in x 4g brass screws	
1 box	1in x 8g screws	
1 box	1½in x 10g screws	
1 box	1½in x 8g screws	
1 box	2in x 8g screws	
20	3in x 8g screws	
20	4in x 8g screws	
8	125 x 10g deck screws	
2	6in 'T' hinges black japanned	Roof vent
	Grey paint spray for hinges	
2	12in galvanised 'T' hinges	Door
1	Door bolt	
1	Automatic vent opener	
	Exterior grade wood adhesive	
2.5 litres	Timber treatment (Sadolin Classic Light oak)	
30 panes	Glass 610 x 610mm	
2 panes	Glass 1422 x 730mm Dutchlyte	Door and roof vent
38	'Z' clips	Glazing
1 sheet	210 x 260mm thin metal sheet	Glazing supports
2	Mini brackets	

This list is for guidance only – it is not a definitive list.

won't be cheaper than an off-the-shelf aluminium one, but it will be better-suited to your own personal requirements. Its dimensions will be dictated by the sizes in which horticultural glass comes, but if you can cut glass then any size is possible.

The base for the greenhouse should be level or have a slight fall towards the door end. It seems most popular these days to have a solid base, although many gardeners still favour a soil base. The choice is yours. Our greenhouse was built onto a paved area that was uneven with considerable slopes in various directions. To compensate for this the greenhouse was built onto a plinth of 100 x 50mm treated timber that was shaped to fit the contours of the paving. If the greenhouse is to have an earth base, a concrete foundation of some type will be needed.

Procedure

The first thing you need to do is to establish the exact dimensions of your greenhouse, which will depend on the number of panes of glass and the size of the beading used to separate it, since these dictate the spacing of the rafters and uprights. Horticultural glass comes in various sizes but the one used for our greenhouse is 610 x 610 x 3mm, with the glass separated by 8 x 8mm bead nailed to the support timbers. The overall size of the greenhouse is approximately 1950 x 1950mm.

Tools
- Universal hard point saw
- Chop saw
- Jigsaw
- Extension lead
- RCD (or safety plug)
- Belt sander
- Electric planer
- Mini (110mm) angle grinder
- Mains-powered electric drill with hammer action
- Drill/driver
- Twist drill bits
  2mm
  5mm
  6mm
  10mm
- Masonry drill bits
  10mm
- Screw-sink and plug cutter
- Flat drill bits
  16mm
- Screwdriver bits
  Posi (PZ) No 2
  Posi (PZ) No 3
  Square No 2
- 4mm flat tip hand-operated screwdriver
- Hammer
- Lump hammer
- Workbenches
- Clamps
- Spirit level
- Try square
- Combination square
- Pencil
- Tape measure
- Sliding bevel
- 25mm (1in) chisel
- Mallet
- Electricians' bolster (55mm)
- Tin shears
- Step ladder
- Mastic gun
- Safety glasses
- Gloves
- Dust mask
- Ear defenders

Gauges

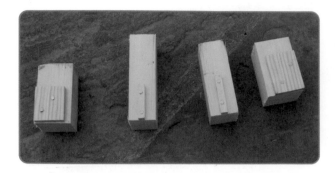

1 The spacing of the upright timbers needs to be very accurate. To help with this make gauge blocks for each of them: the corner uprights are 44 x 44mm PSE and the inner uprights are 33 x 44mm PSE.

Cut two short (75mm) lengths of 44 x 44mm PSE and two of 33 x 44mm PSE. Nail a short length of 8 x 8mm bead to the centre of the 33mm face of the 33 x 44mm PSE to form two inner gauges.

Nail a length of 32 x 8mm bead to the edge of each length of 44 x 44mm PSE, so that one edge of the bead is resting flush with one edge of the 44 x 44mm PSE to form two corner gauges.

Use small galvanised nails, *ie* 25 x 0.8mm wire nails, and drill 2mm holes in the bead to stop it splitting when the nails are driven in.

These four blocks will act as gauges for the spacing of the structural timbers.

2 Cut three glass gauges, from a length of 38 x 18mm batten, to represent the width of the glass. The glass is 610mm wide, to which you need to add 4mm to allow a little room for expansion – the gauges therefore need to be 614mm long. However, if you're very confident of your measuring ability add only 2mm or 3mm to the glass width rather than 4mm. This will create a tighter fit for the glass.

Write something on the gauges so that they aren't accidentally used for another job – '614' or 'gauge' would do. We'll call it the '614' gauge.

3 Lay the two inner gauges, two corner gauges and the '614' gauges out to give the overall size of one side of the greenhouse.

4 Mark their positions onto a length of 75 x 25mm PSE – this sill template will eventually be the back window sill but will also be used as a template for the construction. Leave sufficient wood at each end to form the corners of the sill. Use a try square to make these marks more accurate and to extend them if necessary.

5 Set a combination square to the depth of the gauge blocks (44mm) and mark on the length

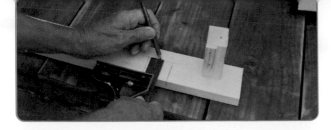

of 75 x 25mm PSE the exact depth of the notch needed to fit the 44 x 44mm and 33 x 44mm timbers.

6 Saw along these marks to the mark along the back made using the combination square. Use a chisel to remove the unwanted timber. Don't try to remove all the timber in one go – make the first incision with your chisel about halfway along the timber to be cut out; then use the chisel along the back line of the notch.

7 Your length of 75 x 25mm will now have four notches cut in it – make sure the 44mm and 33mm gauges fit into each of them. This piece of timber with four notches will serve as a template in the construction of the end frames.

The plinth

Our greenhouse is set onto a plinth of 100 x 50mm treated timber. This separates its untreated timber from the ground, acts as a soleplate, and can be used to level the base if necessary.

1 Use the sill template to cut the 100 x 50mm pressure treated timber to length. Cut the back and front pieces to the same length as the distance between the outside of the two end notches of the sill template. Cut the two side pieces 75mm shorter than the back and front to allow for the width of the end plinth and still allow for a little to trim to length later.

Lay these plinth pieces in place and check for level. If they aren't level, trim (scribe) them so that they're level when resting on the ground. The excess timber was removed using an electric planer.

2 Start levelling from the highest area. You need to prop the 100 x 50mm timber at the lowest point so that it's level with the highest point.

TIP *Using a piece of timber the same thickness as the maximum gap between the ground and the bottom of a levelled piece of timber, make a mark on the plinth indicating where it needs to be planed or sawn off to level it.*

3 Saw or plane each length of the plinth to fit the ground. Then check that the edge is square; if it isn't, correct it.

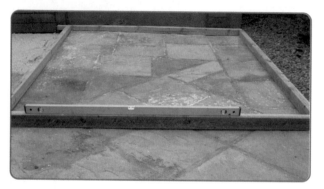

4 Check all the timbers are level and aligned with each other. Label them so that they can be reassembled in the correct order later.

5 The cut and planed sections must be treated to prevent decay. When this has been done put the treated timber to one side to dry. Treat it a few more times if possible.

The angle of the roof

Choose the most suitable pitch angle for the roof. It may need to match other buildings or it may simply be a matter of taste. The angle of pitch of a roof can be found using a sliding bevel (See the kennel project in Chapter 2). The angle cut for the apex of our greenhouse was 38° to match other buildings. Set this angle on the chop saw or on a sliding bevel. It will be used to cut the angle on the rafters and uprights.

TIP *Mark a piece of timber with the correct angle and write on it what it is – then if the sliding bevel is used for another job or accidentally dropped it can be easily reset to the correct angle.*

Height

The height of the walls will be dictated by the glass size, the depth of the timber-clad walls and the height needed for the door. For our greenhouse it worked out to 1810mm, that is, two panes of glass and a wall about 600mm deep including the depth of the plinth. This enabled the door to be 1860mm high.

Take care that the overall height of your greenhouse isn't excessive. The overall height of ours measures 2680mm to the top of the roof, which is within planning regulations.

Making the end frames

1 Cut all the pieces of timber that comprise both the end frames, consisting of four pieces of 44 x 44mm PSE 1810mm long to form the corners (cut a 38° angle on the top of each); four pieces of 44 x 44mm PSE 1260mm long to form the rafters (cut a 38° angle on one end of each); and four pieces of 33 x 44mm PSE 2350mm long to act as inner vertical pieces (cut a 38° angle on one end of each).

Lay the back section of the plinth, on its 100mm face, onto a flat base, and lay the timbers of one frame out to form an end piece. Make sure the timbers are level and are also resting on a flat surface.

2 Use the sill template to mark the location of the uprights onto the 100mm face of the plinth so that they can be transferred onto the top (50mm) face of the plinth later.

6 Drill 6mm screw holes in the 50mm face of the plinth so that the screws go into the ends of the four uprights.

3 Move the sill template to the top of the uprights. Check that the corners are square to the plinth (3 x 4 x 5 triangle).

7 Ensure that the ridge section is exactly in the centre of the frame. This can be done by resting a length of 44 x 44mm PSE along the frame and measuring it carefully to check it's central, and aligning the end with the centre of the dummy ridge section. Mark this location so that the dummy ridge can be realigned if necessary.

8 Mark the rafters at the end of the corner pieces so that they can be cut to length. Cut them with a 38° angle.

4 Cut a 100mm length of 100 x 25mm PSE ridge and rest it between the rafters at their apex.

5 Align the rafters with the top of the corner pieces and check the frame is still square and properly aligned.

9 Screw the 44 x 44mm rafter to the 44 x 44mm PSE corner pieces. Drill a 6mm hole in the end of the rafter at such an angle that the screw will go vertically into the end of the corner piece. Counterbore the hole to allow the screw head to sit below the surface. Drive the screw in, making sure the corner piece stays in place. Do the same for the other rafter.

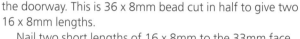

10 Drill a 6mm hole in the top of both rafters so that the screws will go into the 100 x 25mm PSE dummy ridge piece. Screw both rafters to the dummy ridge piece, ensuring that they stay aligned with the bottom of it.

11 Use the sill template to align the inner uprights.

12 Mark and cut the inner uprights to length and screw them into place on the side plate using 125mm x 10g deck screws. Use a 16mm flat bit to counterbore the screw holes so that the screws penetrate further into the timber framework. Screw the 33 x 44mm inner uprights to the rafters.

TIP *Use both your sill template and your two inner gauges and two corner gauges as guides to check that the uprights are in the correct locations.*

---

13 The end frame with the door is constructed in the same way, the only difference being the glass beading on the two uprights that form

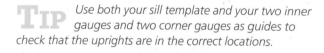

the doorway. This is 36 x 8mm bead cut in half to give two 16 x 8mm lengths.

Nail two short lengths of 16 x 8mm to the 33mm face of a 75mm length of 33 x 44mm PSE to make two door gauge blocks, and build the second (front) end frame on top of the first one in the same way and using the same sill template.

14 The frames should be robust enough to be stood up, but support them well with props clamped or screwed into place. Check that the plinth on both frames is level. Note that standing the frames up is a two-person job.

15 Lower the frames and lay them back on the area on which they were built. Screw offcuts of 44 x 44mm PSE ridge supports at the apex of the rafters so that when the ridge is rested into place the bottom of it will align with the bottom of the rafters.

Stand, then prop the end frames back into place and check that the plinths are level. Use the 100 x 50mm side plinths to space the end frames about the correct distance apart.

Making the side frames

1 With the end frames in place and approximately the correct distance apart, the sill template for the side frames can be made. Rest a length of 75 x 25mm PSE along one side of the greenhouse, between the two end frames. This is to be used to establish the exact length of the greenhouse.

2 Rest in place the two inner gauges with 8 x 8mm bead on them, using the '614' gauge as a guide. The 36 x 8mm glass bead at the ends needs to overlap the 36 x 8mm bead on the corner pieces of the back end frame.

3 When the length of the greenhouse has been established, cut a length of timber to act as a gauge for the internal length (write on it 'inside template'). This can be used to get the correct length at the base and the apex.

4 Cut the two side plinth pieces to length using the inside template as a guide. Rest them in place and check that they align with the front and back plinths and are still level.

angle cut on one end, onto the corner pieces at each end of one side. These are a temporary support for the wall plate. Adjust the height of the temporary support until the top of the wall plate is level with the top of the corner upright.

2 Draw a line at the top of the temporary support to mark the location of the bottom of the wall plate.

3 Drill 6mm holes in the end frame corner pieces for the

5 To add a little more stability fit the 100 x 25mm ridge into place. To do this cut the ridge to length, about 250mm longer than the inside template. Then remove the short dummy lengths of 100 x 25mm PSE from the apexes of the end frames and rest the new ridge into the slot between the rafters, resting it on the ridge supports fixed earlier (page 166). Align it flush at the front apex. Screw the ridge into place at the front using the original screw holes.

Use the inside template to find the correct location for the back apex on the ridge and screw this into place. Remove the ridge supports.

Check that the framework is upright – push it upright and prop it in place if necessary.

Safety Fitting the ridge is a two-person job. Use step ladders and set them up safely.

Fitting the wall plate

The wall plate is the piece of 44 x 33mm PSE timber that runs from back to front supported by the inner uprights. It supports the rafters and is set at an angle to make it easier to fit these. Cut two wall plates to the same length as the inside template.

1 Clamp an offcut of 44 (or 34) x 44mm PSE, with a 38°

screws that fix the wall plate to them, taking care to avoid the screws that hold the rafters to the upright. Use the inside template to mark a length of 34 x 44mm PSE and cut to this length to form the wall plate.

4 Rest the wall plate into place on the two temporary supports and, using 4in x 8g screws, fix it into place through the corner pieces of the ends. Fit the wall plate on the other side in the same way.

Fitting the inner uprights

There are four inner 33 x 44mm PSE uprights (two on each side), 1810mm long with a 38° angle on the top, that fit under the wall plate and on top of the 100 x 50mm plinth. Cut these 20mm longer than needed.

1 Clamp a length of 44 x 44mm PSE onto the outside face of each corner post to align the inner uprights (upright guide). Rest the pre-cut inner uprights into place so that the front of each is touching the upright guide. Clamp this into place and mark the bottom of the inner upright where it touches the 100 x 50mm plinth. Mark and cut the other inner upright for this side and the other two for the other side in the same way.

2 Set up the two inner gauges and two corner gauges to mark the location of the inner timbers onto the plinth and the wall plate.

3 Remove the plinth and drill 6mm holes in its 50mm face for the screws that will fix the inner timbers. Hold the timbers firmly into place and drive one 5in x 12g screw into each.

4 Carefully stand the frame upright. Clamp it in place so that the inner uprights are resting onto the upright guide. Screw down through the wall plate into the tops of the inner timbers.

5 The plinth can now be fitted together by screwing through its front and back pieces into the two side sections using 5in x 12g screws.

The roof

Fixing the roof is a matter of cutting and fitting four 1260mm-long 44 x 33mm PSE rafters with a 38° angle on one end of each.

1 Measure the distance between the inner uprights and mark this distance onto the 100 x 25mm ridge board. Drill a 6mm hole at the centre of these marks and use 2in x 8g screws to screw the angled end of one rafter into place through the hole. Take care that the bottom of the angle, at the top of the rafter, is aligned with the bottom of the ridge board.

2 When the rafter has been screwed into place on the ridge, mark where it needs to be cut off at its other end (foot). Use a straight edge, resting on the outside of the plinth and the wall plate, as a guide. The glass will cover the foot of the rafter so it must be flush with the upright.

Remove the rafter and cut it to length. Check that it fits the other side. If it does it can then be used as a template to cut the other three rafters. Use a try square to mark its alignment on the other side of the ridge board.

Screw the rafter into place at the ridge and screw its foot to the wall plate so that it's aligned perfectly with the inner upright.

3 Drill a 6mm hole through the top of the opposite rafter and screw it into place, taking care that both rafters are aligned. Fix the other rafters in the same way.

4 When all the rafters have been screwed into place the frame will be quite sturdy. Saw the end of the ridge to length.

5 Check that the greenhouse frame is square and level and fix the plinth if necessary – frame fixings are ideal for this. Use a twist drill bit to drill the correct size hole for the fixing through the wood, and a masonry bit to drill into the base. Drive the plastic plug in so that it's level with the top of the plinth then drive the screw in and tighten it. If the uprights aren't firmly fixed to the plinth use brackets to strengthen the fixings.

Locating the glass

1 The 610 x 610mm panes of glass are held together by 'Z' clips. To establish the length of two panes, fit them together on a flat area using the 'Z' clips and make a glass length template exactly the same length as the two panes. This can be used to assess the fit of the glass.

2 The glass on the roof just overlaps the glass on the wall. Rest a straight edge on top of the rafter to represent the glass.

3 Use the glass length template, pushed up against the bottom of the straight edge, to mark the bottom of the glass on the corner pieces and the inner uprights (this is the point where the sill starts – the bottom of the glass rests on the sill). Repeat this process to mark the sill location all round the greenhouse.

The sills

Cut the notches on the two side sills using the same method as suggested on page 161. Take care to leave sufficient timber on the ends to create the joins at the corners. The sill on the front is separated by the door.

1 The sills need a slight chamfer to allow rainwater to run off them. To achieve this, mark a line on the front (25mm face) of the sill, about 4mm down from the top. Draw a line on the top (75mm) face of the sill that joins up the backs of the notches.

2 Use an electric planer to create the slight chamfer demarcated by the lines just drawn. Chamfer all the sills in this way.

3 The corners of the sills are mitred but they could be butted together – the greenhouse will be exposed to all sorts of weather and it may be that a mitre won't remain a tight fit throughout its life. Cutting the mitre is easier to do using a chop saw but it can be done by hand. The mark for the cut is made from the angle of the corner post.

4 The sills don't have to be made in one piece. They could be joined at the inner uprights, either by cutting a 45° angle on the two ends or using a butt joint.

5 The sills are fixed onto battens fitted to the uprights. On our greenhouse 50 x 50mm battens (deck spindles) were used, but 50 x 25mm sawn timber (treated or not) would be ideal. Cut the fixing battens to length using the sill as a gauge. They should fit snugly between the notches in the sill.

TIP *Mark each batten so that it can be matched up with the appropriate sill – they may be slightly different sizes.*

6 It's important that the sill is the same height all around the greenhouse. If it isn't the glass won't fit. To help achieve this, cut a length of wood as a gauge for the sill height and use it as each sill is fitted. Hold the gauge in place and rest the sill onto it at each upright. Mark the exact location of the bottom of the sill.

The centre batten can be screwed through the inner uprights.

7 Mark the thickness of the sill support batten below the sill height mark and find the centre of this rectangle by drawing the diagonals. Drill a 6mm hole at this point.

10 The other two battens are skew screwed to the uprights. Drill a hole at a suitable angle in the end of each. Screw the battens to the underside of the sill so that they're located exactly between the notches. Any holes made in the corner posts will be hidden when the cladding is added.

11 Clamp the sill with the battens screwed to it to the centre (previously fixed) batten, and locate it using the sill height gauge.

8 Screw the sill support batten into place.

TIP *When you're driving in the skew screws they'll tend to lift the sill out of place. To avoid this, clamp an offcut of timber above the sill as well as clamping the sill to the uprights.*

9 Drill two 5mm screw holes in the batten and fix it to the sill using 2in x 8g screws (or some other suitable length if narrower battens are being used).

12 The mitred corners should be screwed and glued into place.

The door opening

Before the door can be built the 44 x 44mm PSE head needs to be fitted between the two inner uprights at the front. Decide on the height of door you want. In our greenhouse it was arranged to be at the level that the two panes of glass reached to from the sill. This gave a door height of 1870mm.

1 Cut the head piece for the doorway to length and mark its location on the frame. Drill the 5mm screw holes, two in each end to stop the head twisting, and clamp, screw and glue the head into place.

2 At some stage the plinth will need to be sawn off in the doorway to allow easy access. Check that the plinth is screwed down to the base (see page 168) and, if you deem it necessary, add a bracket to each side of the doorway to secure the foot of the door uprights to it.

Fitting glass bead

The glass is fitted between lengths of 8 x 8mm and 36 x 8mm bead and set into silicon mastic. A cover strip of 32 x 4mm 'D' shaped bead was screwed to the 8 x 8mm and 36 x 8mm bead to hold the glass in place.

Do *not* glue the bottom 200mm of the 8 x 8mm glass beads on the rafters – a glass retaining strip will need to be fitted under these later.

1 Nail and glue 8 x 8mm glass bead in the exact centre of the outside 33mm face of the 33 x 44mm PSE inner uprights and the 33 x 44mm rafters, using 25 x 1.8mm galvanised wire nails. Use a combination square to ensure the beads are central and use the '614' gauge to ensure they're the correct distance apart (if the greenhouse isn't quite upright or square the inner uprights may come closer together).

TIP *Drill 2mm holes in the bead to stop it being split by the nails.*

2 The corners, and the top of the end rafters, have 36 x 8mm bead to hold the glass. When these beads are applied ensure that the beads on the side face of the 44 x 44mm PSE forming the greenhouse corner pieces are flush with the edge of the corner pieces, and that those on the top of the end 44 x 44mm PSE rafters are flush with the outside face of the rafters – the 36 x 8mm bead on the sides will overlap these. Whilst doing this ensure that the glass length template still fits between the glass beads.

3 Cut an angle on this bead so that it fits to the ridge.

4 Nail and glue it into place in the same way as the 8 x 8mm bead.

TIP *If the nails are kept close to the edge of the 36 x 8mm bead nearest the glass they'll be hidden by the cover strip that holds the glass in place.*

5 Apply 36 x 8mm bead to the corners at the end so that it overlaps the 36 x 8mm bead already in place.

6 Cut the 36 x 8mm bead for the front of the rafters to a 38° angle so that it meets at both apexes. Glue and nail it into place.

7 The glass bead around the doorframe is formed by cutting a length of 36 x 8mm bead in half to form two beads approximately 18 x 8mm. Use a universal hard point saw.

8 The length of the 18 x 8mm strip produced in Step 7 is important. It needs to reach 10mm below the top of the two panes of glass in the front. This is to allow for the 'Z' clip overlap of the next pane of glass.

Mark 10mm from one end of the glass length template. Rest the template on the front sill and mark this line on the doorframe. This will give the length of the 18 x 8mm bead. Cut the bead to length and nail and glue it into place, using the glazing template to ensure it fits.

Cut two lengths of 8 x 8mm bead to fit above the 18 x 8mm bead so that it's level with the inside face of the bead. Using ¾in x 4g brass screws, fix a length of Scotia above the door, level with the marks you've just made. The glass above the door will rest on this.

Fitting the cladding

When all the beading has been fitted the walls below the sill can be clad. The cladding material is a matter of choice. On our greenhouse it was TGV 13 x 100mm, but you might decide on feather-edge or shiplap horizontal cladding (see Chapter 5 for details), or any one of many other options.

1 Measure the height of the wall to assess how long the planks need to be. They don't need to touch the ground, as the skirting will hide the ends, and if they do the end grain will soak up moisture and will rot. The skirting, on the other hand, is sacrificial – if it gets wet and rots it can be easily replaced.

Rest the planks across the width of the area to find how much material needs to be removed from the edges of the cladding at either end. Try to remove about the same amount from each end plank to give a balanced appearance.

2 When deciding on the width of the corner planks take into consideration the amount that the cladding needs to

overlap at the corners. Hold a length of cladding in place and mark it to show the amount that needs to be removed.

3 Use a combination square to define the area to be removed. It can be cut off using a universal hard point saw or a jigsaw, or it can be planed off.

4 Nail the end plank into place through its front face. If this is done with oval nails they can be driven below the surface using a nail punch.

5 Proceed with fixing the other cladding planks, leaving a space of 1mm or 2mm between them to allow for expansion when they get wet. TGV can be held into place using clips that fit into the groove and are nailed to the support frame. The nails can be driven home using a nail punch. Do not glue the cladding into place.

TIP *If the groove in the TGV is too shallow for the clip it may be necessary to drive the clip further in. Use a large screwdriver to do this.*

5a If you fit the TGV cladding through its tongue instead then there's no need for a clip. Drill a small hole for the 25mm galvanised oval nail, hammer the nail into place and use a punch to drive it below the surface.

TIP *Use a screwdriver to keep the planks 1mm or 2mm apart to allow for expansion.*

6 When a few planks have been fixed into place, check the measurement from these to the end of the run to make sure it's the same at top and bottom. If it isn't, adjust the next few planks until the measurements are equal.

7 Finish the run, and mark and cut the last plank so that it fits. This will also have to be nailed through its front face.

Making the door

The door can be made and fitted at any stage after the main construction is completed.

1 Measure the opening for the door and cut two pieces of 44 x 44mm PSE the full height of the opening less 10mm. These side pieces are called the stiles.

Next measure the width of the opening and cut three crosspieces of 44 x 44mm to that length less the thickness of the two stiles (88mm). These are for the head and sole (bottom rail) of the door and the middle division.

Finally cut two pieces of 44 x 33mm PSE the same length as the crosspieces. These are the cladding supports.

Take care to get all your cuts square – if they aren't then the door won't be square either!

Lay out the four main components (the two stiles, the head and the sole) onto a flat and level work area, such as a pair of workbenches. Sash clamps are ideal for holding the doorframe in place, but temporary clamps can be made using timber offcuts and wedges.

2 When all the corners have been aligned, mark the location of the head and sole pieces onto the stiles so that the location of the screw holes can be established. Drill the 6mm holes in the stiles – two at each location – with a screw sink, to accept wooden plugs later (see Chapter 1).

3 Glue, clamp, and screw one 3in x 10g screw into each corner. Check that the diagonals of the door remain the same – if they're not, push the door into shape. Then drive in the remaining four screws.

4 Use glue and 3in x 8g screws to fix the 33mm face of the 44 x 33mm PSE cladding support into place on the sole piece of the door. Take care that it sits flush with the inside of the door to allow the cladding to be flush with the outside of the door. Glue and screw this support member through the stiles as well as to the sole plate. Allow the glue to set.

5 Hold the door in place in the opening and prop it up or clamp it to the head of the doorframe. Mark the location of the sills on either side onto the stiles. Lay the door back down onto the work area and rest the middle length of 44 x 44mm PSE in place at the bottom sill mark and mark around it.

6 Lay the 44 x 33mm PSE cladding support in place and mark around it to show the location of the screw holes.

7 Drill the 6mm screw holes in both stiles and drill two 5mm holes in the 33mm face of the cladding support. Drill screw sink holes in the holes through the stiles – these will be plugged later. Apply the glue and screw the middle piece of 44 x 44mm into place.

8 Screw and glue the cladding support piece into place, checking that it's flush with the inside of the door stiles.

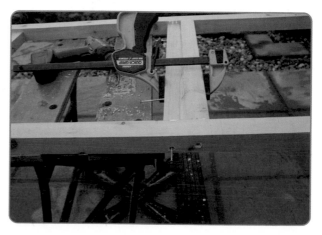

Cladding the door

1 Cut the cladding to length, leaving a 1mm gap at either end for expansion. Lay it in place and mark the amount to be cut from one side piece.

TIP *If the cladding is to be nailed through the tongue, remove the groove.*

2 Use a combination square to mark this line along the side and cut the cladding to width using a saw or a plane – the small amount that needs to be removed could easily be planed off.

3 Plane a slight chamfer on the edge of the cladding to match the 'V' on the other lengths.

4 The cladding can be fixed on the tongue side by secret nailing into the support batten through the tongue, as suggested on page 174.

Hanging the door

For various reasons it was decided to hang the door on our greenhouse so that it opened inwards against one of the sections of staging, but it can be fitted to open outwards if you so desire. Galvanised 'T' hinges were used. If black japanned hinges are used they'll need to be painted to stop them rusting.

Before starting, check that the door fits, and if necessary plane or sand it until it does. Do not make it a tight fit – it doesn't matter if there's some ventilation around it, and it will be exposed to constant changes in conditions so will need room to expand and contract.

5 Mark and cut the final piece of cladding.

6 This will need to be nailed into place, but small oval nails driven below the surface won't be easy to see.

7 Cut and fit a 75 x 25mm sill in the same way as for all the other sills. Glue and screw it to the middle length of 44 x 44mm PSE.

1 Clamp the door to the top of the door opening. Fit a spacer (two layers of thin card) so that it isn't a tight fit.

2 Fit cardboard spacers between the frame and the door on the hinge side. Align the hinges with one side of the doorframe so that they can be screwed to the head or sole of the door, and screw them into place on the frame uprights using 1½in x 10g screws. On our door the hinges

8 Sand off all pencil marks and treat the timber, taking care to treat the exposed end grains.

were wide enough to allow it to overlap at the top of the door. This overlap acts as a doorstop so that the door doesn't swing beyond the frame when it's shut.

TIP *Drill 2mm pilot holes for the screws.*

---

3 Screw the hinges to the door.

Glazing the greenhouse

There seemed at first to be three glazing methods that might be employed: putty, acrylic glazing mastic, or low modulus silicon glazing mastic. However, putty needs to be applied over paint, not stain, while acrylic mastic required a dry day or two to use it and couldn't be covered with a wooden strip. Which left low modulus silicon mastic as the only viable option.

See chapter 1 for further details on glazing and glass cutting.

1 If you don't feel capable of cutting glass make a hardboard template that's a good but loose fit in the opening and ask your glass supplier to cut it for you. The supplier will ask what the glass is for. This is because it's up to him to ensure that you use the correct, safe glass. As yours is for a horticultural purpose, horticultural glass is satisfactory. However, you may feel it safer to use safety glass. On our greenhouse a hardboard template was made for the glass in the door and the glass was cut by the supplier.

2 Our greenhouse design called for some form of glazing support clips for the glass on the roof. These aren't commercially available but they can be made from thin aluminium or copper sheet.

Start by cutting strips from the sheet using tin snips or a mini angle grinder. If using an angle grinder clamp the sheet under a suitable straight edge and run the grinder along it as a guide.

Safety Wear gloves and safety glasses.

Ridge glass support bars

Fitting an angled glazing bar along the ridge to support the glass isn't essential but it does enhance both the waterproofing and appearance of your greenhouse.

3 The strips needed to be two different widths – 32mm for the central rafters where they fitted under the 8 x 8mm glass bars, and 12mm for the side rafters where they fitted alongside the 38 x 8mm beads.

1 The glazing bars are made from lengths of 50 x 25mm PSE with a 38° angle cut along one 25mm face. This can be done using a planer. Cut the bars to length so that they fit between the rafters and plane the angle on the top. Drill two 5mm screw holes in each bar to fix it to the ridge.

4 In order to bend one end of each strip to form a 'U' shape to support the glass, clamp the strip under the blade of a 55mm bolster and onto a workbench, leaving about 12mm poking out. Then gently hammer the strip around the edge of the bolster to form a 'U'.

TIP *The bars can be drilled in batches of three by clamping them together.*

2 Clamp and screw the bars into place using 1½in x 8g screws. Take care that the angle doesn't protrude above the rafters.

5 Use the glass length template to find the required location of the support clips. Nail these into place. The 32mm-wide support strip can be nailed into place through the 8 x 8mm glass bar. The 12mm-wide strip should be nailed into place directly through the strip.

The ridge cap

A cap is needed on top of the ridge to prevent rain from getting to the join where the glass meets the ridge. It consists of a length of 75 x 25mm PSE with the top angled a little to shed the water.

1 Cut the 75 x 25mm PSE to length so that it's 100mm longer than the ridge. Plane an angle of about 20° along each edge of the top 75mm face.

Draw lines to mark the area to be planed off before starting work. For the ridge these were 23mm in from the edge on the 75mm face and 10mm down the 25mm faces.

It isn't necessary to cut these angles but they do help shed water from the ridge cap.

2 Find the centre of the ridge cap. A combination square is ideal for this.

3 Drill five evenly spaced 5mm screw holes for the fixing screws along this centre line. Either use the screw sink to counterbore these holes for wooden plugs, or countersink them ready to be filled with external wood filler later.

4 Hold a short length of 75 x 25mm PSE against the centre of the ridge cap to represent the ridge. Cut a positioning gauge (or set the combination square) that can be used to check the alignment of the ridge cap with the ridge when it's set in place.

5 Clamp the ridge cap into place using the positioning gauge and screw it down to the top of the ridge using 2in x 8g screws.

6 If a roof vent is being fitted it will be necessary to remove two areas of timber from the underside of the ridge to allow it to sit over the hinges. Fit the hinges on the top (25mm face) of the ridge so that they align with the roof vent side pieces. Hold the ridge cap in place and mark the location of the hinges.

Fitting the glass and cover strips

Fitting the glass can either proceed now or can be left until more work has been completed. If a roof vent is being fitted the glazing will need to be completed later, as access will be needed to the vent through the roof. However, the cover strips for the rafters that the roof vent closes onto will need to be fitted before the vent, but they can be removed when necessary and refitted when the glazing is completed.

7 Drive a chisel in around the edges of the area to be removed.

8 Holding the chisel at a low angle, make a series of cuts along the marked area to approximately the depth required. This will cut flakes of timber which can be flicked out later.

9 Clean out the area and try a hinge in it to see if sufficient wood has been removed.

Safety This is a two-person job. Always wear gloves when handling glass.

1 The glass is held in place with a cover strip of 30 x 4mm 'D' section bead (stripwood) screwed to the glass bead using ¾in x 4g brass screws.

Drill 3mm screw holes in the cover strips so that the screws go into the 8mm or 38mm glass bead.

10 A drip groove or drip beads could be added to the ridge cap to make it an even better rainwater shield. A length of beading stuck or nailed along the underside of the ridge cap would be ideal, or a groove could be sawn out using a bench saw.

For the 8 x 8mm bead the screws will be in the centre of the strip. Where the strips fix to the 38 x 8mm bead, at the corners and the apex, the holes will need to be close to one edge so that the screws go into the bead.

2 Cut the cover strips to length so that they cover the full length of the rafters or uprights. Where they fit along the front and back apexes cut them at the appropriate angle to fit at the top and bottom.

TIP *The cover strips can be joined either with a butt joint or by cutting a 45° angle where the two ends meet.*

3 Remove the cover strip and label it so that it can be returned to the same place the correct way up. Apply a thin bead of low modulus silicon glazing mastic to the area that the glass will fit against and push the glass onto it.

4 Hold the glass in place while silicon mastic is applied to the area where the glass joins the glass bead.

5 Refit the cover strip and force any excess mastic under it. Remove any unwanted mastic as soon as possible. To do this put on a rubber glove, dip your index finger in washing-up liquid, and use this to smooth the mastic into the corners between the glass and the bead or cover strip.

Building the roof vent

An opening vent isn't an essential feature for the greenhouse but will be useful. It can, however, be added later, though retrofitting will involve removing the ridge cap and some of the glass from the roof, and glass which has been sealed with silicon mastic is very hard to remove.

Like the glass for the door, the glass for the vent is too large to cut from a 610 x 610mm sheet.

The inner section of the vent, which fits between the rafters, is made using 50 x 25mm PSE. The upper section, which fits over the glass bead and cover strip, uses 75 x 25mm PSE for the sides and 50 x 25mm PSE for the top.

1 Cut a length of 44 x 44mm PSE to fit between the two rafters where the roof vent is to go, and glue and nail a length of 8 x 8mm bead to one face. Then fix it in place

between the rafters so that the top of the pane of glass below the vent will rest onto it when the bottom of the glass is aligned with the other panes and its top is against the 8 x 8mm bead. (The 8 x 8mm bead could be added after the 44 x 44mm crosspiece has been fitted.)

2 Cut three 585mm lengths of 50 x 25mm PSE, two for the top and one for the bottom of the vent. These need to fit between the rafters on either side of the vent. Cut a 40° angle along the length of one 25mm face on two of them. This can be done by marking the angles on the end and planing the wood off.

3 Clamp together the two pieces with the angles cut on them so that the angles are flush with each other. Mark the overlap on the lower piece. This is the area the glass will rest on at the top of the vent. The piece with the glass line marked on it forms the top part of the inner section of the vent. The angle rests against the ridge.

4 Cut two 545mm lengths of 50 x 25mm PSE for the side pieces. When screwed to the top and bottom pieces these make a frame that fits between the rafters and against a length of 44 x 44mm PSE that the lower pane of glass rests on (Step 1).

Drill 5mm screw holes in the ends of the top angled piece and the bottom non-angled piece of 50 x 25mm PSE. These need to be drilled so that the screws go into the ends of the two 50 x 25mm side pieces. Then screw and glue the frame together using 2½in x 8g screws.

5 Lay the vent frame on a flat surface, check the diagonals to ensure that it's square and allow the glue to set.

6 Check that the frame fits inside the rafters and against the ridge. Sand it to fit if necessary.

9 The glass in the roof vent needs to overlap the fixed pane of glass in the roof by at least 40mm. Cut a length of

7 Set a combination square to the measurement of the glazing line on the angled top of the frame and use it to mark a line down the frame sides.

8 Cut two 700mm-long pieces of 75 x 25mm PSE to form the sides of the upper section of the vent. Cut a 40° angle on one end of each. Align the 40° angle with the angle on the top of the inner section and the glazing line drawn in Step 7 and clamp it into place.

bead or timber to represent the total length of the glass from the glazing mark on the top piece to the end of the overlap. Hold this in place and mark the length of the upper section sides. Do the same on the other side – taking care that the angles at the top are aligned. Remove the side pieces and cut them to length. Keep the length of bead as a gauge for cutting the glass.

10 Sand the ends of the upper side pieces.

11 Glue and screw the upper side pieces into place through the inner side pieces, using 1½in x 8g screws. The

screws need to be arranged on either side of the joins to give them more strength. Ensure that they're aligned with the marks for the glass along the side and that the angles on the top are flush.

12 Screw and glue the 50 x 25mm angled top piece into place. Ensure that the angles on the top are flush. Allow the glue to set and try the frame in place. Make any necessary adjustments until it fits.

13 Make up two 10mm-wide glass clips (see page 172). These need to be long enough to overlap the end of the frame by 40mm and provide adequate fixing onto it.

Hingeing the vent

The easiest way to hinge the vent is using 150mm 'T' hinges. These black japanned hinges were sprayed silver to make them more weather-resistant and to make them look like galvanised metal – actual galvanised hinges of the correct size were too chunky for the job.

1 Remove the ridge cap and take care to locate the hinges so that they coincide with the recessed area (see page 180). Screw the hinges into place on the top of the ridge using 1½in x 8g screws. Replace the ridge cap.

2 Rest the vent in place and wedge pieces of card between its sides and the rafters to ensure that there's some space for movement and that the vent is central. Make sure the vent is pushed tight against the ridge and use 1in x 8g stainless steel screws to fix the hinge to the vent. Fit two screws in each hinge and check the vent opens freely. If it doesn't, loosen the screws, wedge the vent so that it will open freely, and then add the rest of the screws.

3 Remove the vent so that it can be glazed. Cut mitres on lengths of glass bead so that they fit into the corners. The bead should be long enough to just touch the glass clip. Drill 2mm holes in the glass bead ready for the screws.

4 Cut the glass to size. Apply silicon mastic to the frame and push the glass into place. Apply more silicon to fill the gap and screw the bead into place using ¾in x 4g brass screws.

Staging

The staging is constructed using 38 x 18mm roofing batten fixed to the uprights of the greenhouse and 75 x 25mm PSE for the front with a length of 38 x 20mm batten fixed to the back of it. The cross battens rest onto these two supports. The level of the staging is a matter of choice: in our greenhouse it was set level with the bottom of the sill. It can be built along both the sides and the back if required.

1 Use 1½in x 8g screws to fix a length of batten to the uprights of the greenhouse so that a section of batten resting on top will be level with the bottom of the sill.

2 Cut a length of 38 x 18mm cross batten to the required width of the staging (455mm). Use this batten as a gauge to determine the location of the front piece. Cut a support leg to length – we used 50 x 50mm decking spindles –

and screw it to the greenhouse plinth and sill supports at one end of the greenhouse using 2½in x 8g screws.

3 Fix another support leg at the other end of the greenhouse the same distance (455mm) from the side.

Cut a length of 75 x 25mm PSE to form the staging front piece. This fits between the ends of the greenhouse. Screw it to the two end support legs.

Cut the other two support legs and screw them into place opposite the inner uprights.

4 Fix lengths of batten between the support legs and align them with the top of the legs. These support the cross battens. They can be screwed to the front piece through the batten so that the screws can't be seen. If required, fit staging to the other side of the greenhouse in the same way.

5 Cut battens to length so that they fit between the front support and the greenhouse wall and rest them in place. A few can be screwed into place if this is deemed necessary.

Skirting

The skirting is fitted to conceal the gap between the ground and the cladding, to hold the latter in place, and to allow the cladding to end 20mm or so above the ground. Because of its proximity to the damp ground it must be regarded as sacrificial and therefore needs to be easily removable.

1 Set the skirting level and, using a piece of wood the same thickness as the amount needed to level it, mark a pencil line along the bottom of the skirting. Cut along this line so that the skirting will fit close to the ground. Scribe all the skirting to fit, ensuring that the corners meet.

2 Cut a mitre on the skirting at each corner.

3 Treat all the skirting, back and front, with a good timber preservative.

4 Screw the skirting into place, leaving the screw heads exposed so that they can be removed when necessary.

Door furniture

Handles were fitted to the inside and outside of the door. The handles chosen were actually designed for cupboards, which meant that the bolts were too short to go through the stile. This problem can be overcome by drilling a counterbore hole or finding longer bolts. More details about fitting catches can be found in Chapter 1.

1 A small bolt was fitted simply to allow the door to be bolted shut, not for security

reasons. Use a try square to align the bolt on the door and mark two screw holes. Drill these with a 1mm bit and drive in the screws. Check that the bolt is square to the door and screw in the other screws.

2 Mark where the bolt touches the doorframe and drill two holes at this point using a 4mm bit. These can be merged together to form a single hole large enough for the bolt.

TIP *Drill two 2mm holes first to act as a guide for the larger bit.*

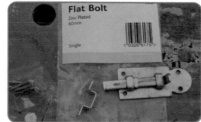

USEFUL CONTACTS

Adhesives and mastics

Evode – suppliers of FlashBand
www.evode.co.uk

Henkel – adhesives and silicon mastic
www.loctite.co.uk

Animal care

Blue Cross – kennel and hutch sizes
www.bluecross.org.uk

RSPB - information about nesting boxes
www.rspb.org.uk

Tiggywinkles – animal hospital for hedgehogs
www.sttiggywinkles.org.uk

First Aid and safety

DTI – safety leaflets
www.dti.gov.uk/consumers/fact-sheets

Red Cross – First Aid kit
www.redcross.org.uk

ROSPA – safety and accident prevention
www.rospa.com

St John Ambulance
08700 104950
www.sja.org.uk

Fixings

Abru Joyner – brackets
www.abru.co.uk

Expamet – joist hangers and building metalwork
www.expamet.co.uk

FastenMaster – deck screws
www.ajsmith.uk.com

Fischer – frame fixings
www.fischer.co.uk

Metpost – post spurs and finials
www.metpost.co.uk

Rawl – masonry fixings – www.rawlplug.co.uk

Screwfix – screws and fixings
www.screwfix.co.uk

General advice

B&Q – www.diy.com
www.diydata.com
wwwdiydoctor.org.uk

Focus www.focusdiy.co.uk
Homebase – www.homebase.co.uk

Tony Lush – general details and information
www.tonylush.co.uk

Glass

Glass and Glazing Federation – www.ggf.co.uk

DoubleGlazing UK – www.double-glazing-uk.co.uk

diydata.com
www.diydata.com

Gravel and concrete

www.Hanson.co.uk > garden and landscaping >
complementary products

Paving Expert – www.pavingexpert.com

Greenhouses

GardenAction
www.gardenaction.co.uk

Every Action Counts
www.everyactioncounts.org.uk

Paint and timber preservatives

Arch Timber Protection
01977 714000
www.archtp.com

Cuprinol – timber treatment
www.cuprinol.co.uk

Dulux – paints – www.dulux.co.uk

Hammerite – metal paint
www.hammerite.com

International – garage floor paint
www.international-paints.co.uk

Plasti-kote – spray paint
www.plasti-kote.com

Sadolin – timber treatment – www.sadolin.co.uk

Thermowood – decay-resistant timber
www.finnforest.co.uk

Regulations

Electricity
www.communities.gov.uk
www.napit.org.uk

Planning – www.communities.gov.uk

Water
www.wras.co.uk
www.southernwater.co.uk > resources > faqs > regulations

Timber

B.C. Shake & Shingle Association – cedar shingles
www.bcshakeshingle.com

Finnforest – timber decking
www.finnforest.co.uk

Hales & Co (Drybrook) – timber and building materials
01594 545300

Richard Burbidge – stripwood
www.richardburbidge.co.uk

Timber Decking Association
www.tda.co.uk

Tool suppliers

Bahco – Sandvic hand saws
www.bahco.com

Black & Decker – power tools
www.blackanddecker.co.uk

www.masterplug.com

Trend – screwdriver bits
www.trendmachinery.co.uk

www.stanleyworks.co.uk

Wolfcraft – corner clamps
www.wolfcraft.co.uk

Author:	Tony Lush
Project Manager:	Louise McIntyre
Copy Editor:	Ian Heath
Design/layout:	James Robertson
Illustrations:	Rob Loxston
Index:	Peter Nicholson